MznLnx

Missing Links Exam Preps

Exam Prep for

Understanding Financial Statements

Fraser & Ormiston, 8th Edition

The MznLnx Exam Prep is your link from the texbook and lecture to your exams.
The MznLnx Exam Preps are unauthorized and comprehensive reviews of your textbooks.

All material provided by MznLnx and Rico Publications (c) 2010
Textbook publishers and textbook authors do not particpate in or contribute to these reviews.

MznLnx

Rico
Publications

Exam Prep for Understanding Financial Statements
8th Edition
Fraser & Ormiston

Publisher: Raymond Houge
Assistant Editor: Michael Rouger
Text and Cover Designer: Lisa Buckner
Marketing Manager: Sara Swagger
Project Manager, Editorial Production: Jerry Emerson
Art Director: Vernon Lowerui

Product Manager: Dave Mason
Editorial Assitant: Rachel Guzmanji
Pedagogy: Debra Long
Cover Image: Jim Reed/Getty Images
Text and Cover Printer: City Printing, Inc.
Compositor: Media Mix, Inc.

(c) 2010 Rico Publications
ALL RIGHTS RESERVED. No part of this work covered by the copyright may be reproduced or used in any form or by an means--graphic, electronic, or mechanical, including photocopying, recording, taping, Web distribution, information storage, and retrieval systems, or in any other manner--without the written permission of the publisher.

For more information about our products, contact us at:
Dave.Mason@RicoPublications.com

For permission to use material from this text or product, submit a request online to:
Dave.Mason@RicoPublications.com

Printed in the United States
ISBN:

Contents

CHAPTER 1
Financial Statements: An Overview — 1

CHAPTER 2
The Balance Sheet — 22

CHAPTER 3
Income Statement and Statement of Stockholders Equity — 42

CHAPTER 4
Statement of Cash Flows — 63

CHAPTER 5
A Guide to Earnings and Financial Reporting Quality — 75

CHAPTER 6
The Analysis of Financial Statements — 94

ANSWER KEY — 115

TO THE STUDENT

COMPREHENSIVE

The *MznLnx* Exam Prep series is designed to help you pass your exams. Editors at MznLnx review your textbooks and then prepare these practice exams to help you master the textbook material. Unlike study guides, workbooks, and practice tests provided by the texbook publisher and textbook authors, *MznLnx* gives you **all** of the material in each chapter in exam form, not just samples, so you can be sure to nail your exam.

MECHANICAL

The MznLnx Exam Prep series creates exams that will help you learn the subject matter as well as test you on your understanding. Each question is designed to help you master the concept. Just working through the exams, you gain an understanding of the subject--its a simple mechanical process that produces success.

INTEGRATED STUDY GUIDE AND REVIEW

MznLnx is not just a set of exams designed to test you, its also a comprehensive review of the subject content. Each exam question is also a review of the concept, making sure that you will get the answer correct without having to go to other sources of material. You learn as you go! Its the easiest way to pass an exam.

HUMOR

Studying can be tedious and dry. MznLnx's instructional design includes moderate humor within the exam questions on occassion, to break the tedium and revitalize the brain

Chapter 1. Financial Statements: An Overview

1. _____ are formal records of a business' financial activities.

   _____ provide an overview of a business' financial condition in both short and long term. There are four basic _____:

   1. **Balance sheet**: also referred to as statement of financial position or condition, reports on a company's assets, liabilities, and net equity as of a given point in time.
   2. **Income statement**: also referred to as Profit and Loss statement (or a 'P'L'), reports on a company's income, expenses, and profits over a period of time.
   3. **Statement of retained earnings**: explains the changes in a company's retained earnings over the reporting period.
   4. **Statement of cash flows**: reports on a company's cash flow activities, particularly its operating, investing and financing activities.

   a. Financial statements
   b. Statement of retained earnings
   c. Notes to the Financial Statements
   d. Statement on Auditing Standards No. 70: Service Organizations

2. A _____ is a pool of assets forming an independent legal entity that are bought with the contributions to a pension plan for the exclusive purpose of financing pension plan benefits.

   _____s are important shareholders of listed and private companies. They are especially important to the stock market where large institutional investors like the Ontario Teachers' Pension Plan dominate.

   a. Leveraged buyout
   b. Limited liability company
   c. Leverage
   d. Pension fund

3. _____ refers to an assessment of the viability, stability and profitability of a business, sub-business or project.

   It is performed by professionals who prepare reports using ratios that make use of information taken from financial statements and other reports. These reports are usually presented to top management as one of their bases in making business decisions.

   a. Financial analysis
   b. 529 plan
   c. Value investing
   d. 4-4-5 Calendar

Chapter 1. Financial Statements: An Overview

4. An _____ is a document a company presents at an annual general meeting for approval by its shareholders, or a charitable organization presents its trustees. The report is made up of reports, which may include the following:

- Chairman's report
- CEO's report
- Auditor's report on corporate governance
- Mission statement
- Corporate governance statement of compliance
- Statement of directors' responsibilities
- Invitation to the company's AGM

as well as financial statements including:

- Auditor's report on the financial statements
- Balance sheet
- Statement of retained earnings
- Income statement
- Cash flow statement
- Notes to the financial statements
- Accounting policies

Other information deemed relevant to stakeholders may be included, such as a report on operations for manufacturing firms. In the case of larger companies, it is usually a sleek, colorful, high gloss publication.

The details provided in the report are of use to investors to understand the company's financial position and future direction.

a. Outstanding balance
b. Amortization schedule
c. Accrued liabilities
d. Annual report

5. _____ is the field of accountancy concerned with the preparation of financial statements for decision makers, such as stockholders, suppliers, banks, employees, government agencies, owners, and other stakeholders. The fundamental need for _____ is to reduce principal-agent problem by measuring and monitoring agents' performance and reporting the results to interested users.

_____ is used to prepare accounting information for people outside the organization or not involved in the day to day running of the company.

Chapter 1. Financial Statements: An Overview

a. Financial Accounting
b. 529 plan
c. 4-4-5 Calendar
d. 7-Eleven

6. A _____ is a fungible, negotiable instrument representing financial value. They are broadly categorized into debt securities (such as banknotes, bonds and debentures), and equity securities; e.g., common stocks. The company or other entity issuing the _____ is called the issuer.
   a. Securities lending
   b. Security
   c. Book entry
   d. Tracking stock

7. The U.S. _____ is an independent agency of the United States government which holds primary responsibility for enforcing the federal securities laws and regulating the securities industry, the nation's stock and options exchanges, and other electronic securities markets. The SEC was created by section 4 of the SEC of 1934 (now codified as 15 U.S.C. § 78d and commonly referred to as the 1934 Act.)
   a. 4-4-5 Calendar
   b. 529 plan
   c. 7-Eleven
   d. Securities and Exchange Commission

8. The role of the _____ is to issue accounting standards in the United Kingdom. It is recognised for that purpose under the Companies Act 1985. It took over the task of setting accounting standards from the Accounting Standards Committee (ASC) in 1990.
   a. A Random Walk Down Wall Street
   b. AAB
   c. ABN Amro
   d. Accounting Standards Board

9. _____ or First In, First Out, is an abstraction in ways of organizing and manipulation of data relative to time and prioritization. This expression describes the principle of a queue processing technique or servicing conflicting demands by ordering process by first-come, first-served (FCFS) behaviour: what comes in first is handled first, what comes in next waits until the first is finished, etc.

Thus it is analogous to the behaviour of persons queueing (or 'standing in line', in common American parlance), where the persons leave the queue in the order they arrive, or waiting one's turn at a traffic control signal.

a. 4-4-5 Calendar
b. Penny stock
c. Risk management
d. FIFO

10. The _____ is a private, not-for-profit organization whose primary purpose is to develop generally accepted accounting principles (GAAP) within the United States in the public's interest. The Securities and Exchange Commission (SEC) designated the _____ as the organization responsible for setting accounting standards for public companies in the U.S. It was created in 1973, replacing the Accounting Principles Board and the Committee on Accounting Procedure of the American Institute of Certified Public Accountants. The _____'s mission is 'to establish and improve standards of financial accounting and reporting for the guidance and education of the public, including issuers, auditors, and users of financial information.'

The _____ is not a governmental body.

a. Federal Deposit Insurance Corporation
b. World Congress of Accountants
c. KPMG
d. Financial Accounting Standards Board

11. _____ is a list for goods and materials held available in stock by a business. It is also used for a list of the contents of a household and for a list for testamentary purposes of the possessions of someone who has died. In accounting _____ is considered an asset.
a. A Random Walk Down Wall Street
b. ABN Amro
c. Inventory
d. AAB

12. An _____ is a contract written by a seller that conveys to the buyer the right -- but not the obligation -- to buy (in the case of a call _____) or to sell (in the case of a put _____) a particular asset, such as a piece of property such as, among others, a futures contract. In return for granting the _____, the seller collects a payment (the premium) from the buyer.

For example, buying a call _____ provides the right to buy a specified quantity of a security at a set strike price at some time on or before expiration, while buying a put _____ provides the right to sell.

a. AT'T Mobility LLC
b. Amortization
c. Annuity
d. Option

13. _____ or accounting is the system of recording, verifying, and reporting of the value of assets, liabilities, income, and expenses in the books of account (ledger) to which debit and credit entries (recognizing transactions) are chronologically posted to record changes in value Such financial information is primarily used by lenders, managers, investors, tax authorities and other decision makers to make resource allocation decisions between and within companies, organizations, and public agencies. Accounting has been defined by the AICPA as ' The art of recording, classifying, and summarizing in a significant manner and in terms of money, transactions and events which are, in part at least, of financial character, and interpreting the results thereof.'

Financial accounting is one branch of accounting and historically has involved processes by which financial information about a business is recorded, classified, summarised, interpreted, and communicated; for public companies, this information is generally publicly-accessible.

a. Accountancy
b. A Random Walk Down Wall Street
c. AAB
d. ABN Amro

14. In business and accounting, _____s are everything of value that is owned by a person or company. The balance sheet of a firm records the monetary value of the _____s owned by the firm. The two major _____ classes are tangible _____s and intangible _____s.
a. Asset
b. Accounts payable
c. Income
d. EBITDA

15. In financial accounting, a _____ or statement of financial position is a summary of a person's or organization's balances. Assets, liabilities and ownership equity are listed as of a specific date, such as the end of its financial year. A _____ is often described as a snapshot of a company's financial condition.
a. Statement of retained earnings
b. Statement on Auditing Standards No. 70: Service Organizations
c. Financial statements
d. Balance sheet

16. _____, refers to consumption opportunity gained by an entity within a specified time frame, which is generally expressed in monetary terms. However, for households and individuals, '_____ is the sum of all the wages, salaries, profits, interests payments, rents and other forms of earnings received... in a given period of time.' For firms, _____ generally refers to net-profit: what remains of revenue after expenses have been subtracted.
   a. Annual report
   b. Accrual
   c. Income
   d. OIBDA

17. An _____ is a financial statement for companies that indicates how Revenue is transformed into net income The purpose of the _____ is to show managers and investors whether the company made or lost money during the period being reported.

The important thing to remember about an _____ is that it represents a period of time.

   a. AAB
   b. ABN Amro
   c. A Random Walk Down Wall Street
   d. Income statement

18. _____ are additional notes and information added to the end of the financial statements to supplement the reader with more information. Notes to Financial Statements help explain the computation of specific items in the financial statements as well as provide a more comprehensive assessment of a company's financial condition. Notes to Financial Statements can include information on debt, going concern, accounts, contingent liabilities, or contextual information explaining the financial numbers (e.g. to indicate a lawsuit.)
   a. Financial statements
   b. Statement on Auditing Standards No. 70: Service Organizations
   c. Statement of retained earnings
   d. Notes to the financial statements

Chapter 1. Financial Statements: An Overview 7

19. _____ is the balance of the amounts of cash being received and paid by a business during a defined period of time, sometimes tied to a specific project. Measurement of _____ can be used

- to evaluate the state or performance of a business or project.
- to determine problems with liquidity. Being profitable does not necessarily mean being liquid. A company can fail because of a shortage of cash, even while profitable.
- to generate project rate of returns. The time of _____s into and out of projects are used as inputs to financial models such as internal rate of return, and net present value.
- to examine income or growth of a business when it is believed that accrual accounting concepts do not represent economic realities. Alternately, _____ can be used to 'validate' the net income generated by accrual accounting.

_____ as a generic term may be used differently depending on context, and certain _____ definitions may be adapted by analysts and users for their own uses. Common terms include operating _____ and free _____.

_____s can be classified into:

1. Operational _____s: Cash received or expended as a result of the company's core business activities.
2. Investment _____s: Cash received or expended through capital expenditure, investments or acquisitions.
3. Financing _____s: Cash received or expended as a result of financial activities, such as interests and dividends.

All three together - the net _____ - are necessary to reconcile the beginning cash balance to the ending cash balance. Loan draw downs or equity injections, that is just shifting of capital but no expenditure as such, are not considered in the net _____.

a. Shareholder value
b. Cash flow
c. Corporate finance
d. Real option

20. In accounting, _____ refers to the portion of net income which is retained by the corporation rather than distributed to its owners as dividends. Similarly, if the corporation makes a loss, then that loss is retained and called variously retained losses, accumulated losses or accumulated deficit. _____ and losses are cumulative from year to year with losses offsetting earnings.
a. Matching principle
b. Generally Accepted Accounting Principles
c. Historical cost
d. Retained earnings

Chapter 1. Financial Statements: An Overview

21. In financial accounting, a _____ or statement of cash flows is a financial statement that shows a company's flow of cash. The money coming into the business is called cash inflow, and money going out from the business is called cash outflow. The statement shows how changes in balance sheet and income accounts affect cash and cash equivalents, and breaks the analysis down to operating, investing, and financing activities.
   a. 4-4-5 Calendar
   b. 7-Eleven
   c. 529 plan
   d. Cash flow statement

22. The _____ is one of the basic financial statements as per Generally Accepted Accounting Principles, and it explains the changes in a company's retained earnings over the reporting period. It breaks down changes affecting the account, such as profits or losses from operations, dividends paid, and any other items charged or credited to retained earnings. A retained earnings statement is required by Generally Accepted Accounting Principles (GAAP) whenever comparative balance sheets and income statements are presented.
   a. Notes to the Financial Statements
   b. Financial statements
   c. Statement on Auditing Standards No. 70: Service Organizations
   d. Statement of retained earnings

23. The _____ of 2002 (Pub.L. 107-204, 116 Stat. 745, enacted July 30, 2002), also known as the Public Company Accounting Reform and Investor Protection Act of 2002 and commonly called Sarbanes-Oxley, Sarbox or SOX, is a United States federal law enacted on July 30, 2002 in response to a number of major corporate and accounting scandals including those affecting Enron, Tyco International, Adelphia, Peregrine Systems and WorldCom.
   a. Sarbanes-Oxley Act
   b. Duty of loyalty
   c. Foreign Corrupt Practices Act
   d. Blue sky law

24. _____ is a term used in accounting, economics and finance to spread the cost of an asset over the span of several years.

In simple words we can say that _____ is the reduction in the value of an asset due to usage, passage of time, wear and tear, technological outdating or obsolescence, depletion or other such factors.

In accounting, _____ is a term used to describe any method of attributing the historical or purchase cost of an asset across its useful life, roughly corresponding to normal wear and tear.

Chapter 1. Financial Statements: An Overview

a. Depreciation
b. Deferred financing costs
c. Bottom line
d. Matching principle

25. _____ LLP, based in Chicago, was once one of the 'Big Five' accounting firms among PricewaterhouseCoopers, Deloitte Touche Tohmatsu, Ernst ' Young and KPMG, providing auditing, tax, and consulting services to large corporations. In 2002, the firm voluntarily surrendered its licenses to practice as Certified Public Accountants in the United States after being found guilty of criminal charges relating to the firm's handling of the auditing of Enron, the energy corporation, resulting in the loss of 85,000 jobs. Although the verdict was subsequently overturned by the Supreme Court of the United States, it has not returned as a viable business.

a. Institute of Financial Accountants
b. Information Systems Audit and Control Association
c. Accion USA
d. Arthur Andersen

26. The institution most often referenced by the word '_____' is a public or publicly traded _____, the shares of which are traded on a public stock exchange (e.g., the New York Stock Exchange or Nasdaq in the United States) where shares of stock of _____s are bought and sold by and to the general public. Most of the largest businesses in the world are publicly traded _____s. However, the majority of _____s are said to be closely held, privately held or close _____s, meaning that no ready market exists for the trading of shares.

a. Protect
b. Depository Trust Company
c. Federal Home Loan Mortgage Corporation
d. Corporation

27. While the full name of the Swiss verein is Deloitte Touche Tohmatsu, in 1989 it initially branded itself _____ and then simply Deloitte. In 2003 the rebranding campaign was commissioned by Bill Parrett, the then CEO of DTT, and led by Jerry Leamon, the global Clients and Markets leader.

Deloitte member firms offer services in the following functions, with country-specific variations on their legal implementation (i.e. all operating within a single company or through separate legal entities operating as subsidiaries of an umbrella legal entity for the country.)

a. Fixed income
b. Rate of return
c. Monte Carlo methods
d. Deloitte ' Touche

28. _____ is one of the largest professional services firms in the world. _____ employs over 123,000 people in a global network of member firms spanning over 145 countries. Composite revenues of _____ member firms in 2007 were $19.8 billion USD (17.4% growth from 2006.)
   a. Federal Deposit Insurance Corporation
   b. National Association of State Boards of Accountancy
   c. Texas ratio
   d. KPMG

29. The term _____ usually refers to a company that is permitted to offer its registered securities for sale to the general public, typically through a stock exchange, or occasionally a company whose stock is traded over the counter via market makers who use non-exchange quotation services.

The term '_____' may also refer to a company owned by the government.

   a. First Prudential Markets
   b. Public Company
   c. Corporation
   d. General partnership

30. The _____ (sometimes called 'Peekaboo') is a private-sector, non-profit corporation created by the Sarbanes-Oxley Act, a 2002 United States federal law, to oversee the auditors of public companies. Its stated purpose is to 'protect the interests of investors and further the public interest in the preparation of informative, fair, and independent audit reports'. Although a private entity, the _____ has many government-like regulatory functions, making it in some ways similar to the private Self Regulatory Organizations (SROs) that regulate stock markets and other aspects of the financial markets in the United States.
   a. World Trade Organization
   b. Gamelan Council
   c. Financial Crimes Enforcement Network
   d. Public Company Accounting Oversight Board

31. _____ are the earnings returned on the initial investment amount.

In the US, the Financial Accounting Standards Board (FASB) requires companies' income statements to report _____ for each of the major categories of the income statement: continuing operations, discontinued operations, extraordinary items, and net income.

The _____ formula does not include preferred dividends for categories outside of continued operations and net income.

a. Average accounting return
b. Assets turnover
c. Inventory turnover
d. Earnings per share

32. In business and finance, a _____ (also referred to as equity _____) of stock means a _____ of ownership in a corporation (company.) In the plural, stocks is often used as a synonym for _____s especially in the United States, but it is less commonly used that way outside of North America.

In the United Kingdom, South Africa, and Australia, stock can also refer to completely different financial instruments such as government bonds or, less commonly, to all kinds of marketable securities.

a. Share
b. Procter ' Gamble
c. Margin
d. Bucket shop

33. _____ is the statutory title of qualified accountants in the United States who have passed the Uniform _____ Examination and have met additional state education and experience requirements for certification as a _____. In most U.S. states, only _____s who are licensed are able to provide to the public attestation (including auditing) opinions on financial statements. The exceptions to this rule are Arizona, Kansas, North Carolina and Ohio where, although the '_____' designation is restricted, the practice of auditing is not.

a. Certified General Accountant
b. Certified Public Accountant
c. Chartered Accountant
d. Chartered Certified Accountant

34. The _____ is the former authoritative body of the American Institute of Certified Public Accountants (AICPA.) It was created by the American Institute of Certified Public Accountants in 1959 and issued pronouncements on accounting principles until 1973, when it was replaced by the Financial Accounting Standards Board (FASB.)

The _____ was disbanded in the hopes that the smaller, fully-independent FASB could more effectively create accounting standards.

a. Accounting Principles Board
b. American Accounting Association
c. Upromise
d. Openda

35. _____ plant, and equipment, is a term used in accountancy for assets and property which cannot easily be converted into cash. This can be compared with current assets such as cash or bank accounts, which are described as liquid assets. In most cases, only tangible assets are referred to as fixed.
   a. Remittance advice
   b. Percentage of Completion
   c. Petty cash
   d. Fixed asset

36. In financial accounting, _____s are precautions for which the amount or probability of occurrence are not known. Typical examples are _____s for warranty costs and _____ for taxes the term reserve is used instead of term _____; such a use, however, is inconsistent with the terminology suggested by International Accounting Standards Board.
   a. Provision
   b. Petty cash
   c. Money measurement concept
   d. Momentum Accounting and Triple-Entry Bookkeeping

37. A _____ is a statement required of a United States firm when soliciting shareholder votes. The firm needs to file a _____ with the U.S. Securities and Exchange Commission. This statement is useful in assessing how management is paid and potential conflict-of-interest issues with auditors.
   a. 7-Eleven
   b. Proxy statement
   c. 4-4-5 Calendar
   d. 529 plan

38. _____, in bookkeeping, refers to assets, liabilities, income, and expenses recorded on individual pages of the so called book of final entry or ledger. Changes in _____ value are made by chronologically posting debit (DR) and credit (CR) entries to its page. Examples of _____s are cash, _____s receivable, mortgages, loans, land and buildings, common stock, sales, services provided, wages, and payroll overhead.
   a. Alpha
   b. Option
   c. Accretion
   d. Account

39. _____, also called fair price (in a commonplace conflation of the two distinct concepts), is a concept used in finance and economics, defined as a rational and unbiased estimate of the potential market price of a good, service, or asset, taking into account such objective factors as:

- acquisition/production/distribution costs, replacement costs, or costs of close substitutes
- actual utility at a given level of development of social productive capability
- supply vs. demand

and subjective factors such as

- risk characteristics
- cost of capital
- individually perceived utility

In accounting, _____ is used as an estimate of the market value of an asset (or liability) for which a market price cannot be determined (usually because there is no established market for the asset.) Under GAAP (FAS 157), _____ is the amount at which the asset could be bought or sold in a current transaction between willing parties, or transferred to an equivalent party, other than in a liquidation sale. This is used for assets whose carrying value is based on mark-to-market valuations; for assets carried at historical cost, the _____ of the asset is not used. One example of where _____ is an issue is a College kitchen with a cost of $2 million which was built 5 years ago.

    a. Fair value
    b. 4-4-5 Calendar
    c. 7-Eleven
    d. 529 plan

40. _____ was founded in June 1973 in London and replaced by the International Accounting Standards Board on April 1, 2001. It was responsible for developing the International Accounting Standards and promoting the use and application of these standards.

The _____ was founded as a result of an agreement between accountancy bodies in the following countries:

- Australia (Institute of Chartered Accountants in Australia (ICAA) and the CPA Australia (formerly known as Australian Society of Certified Practising Accountants (ASCPA))

- Canada (Canadian Institute of Chartered Accountants (CICA))

- France (Ordre des Experts Comptable et des Comptables Agrees (Order of Accounting Experts and Qualified Accountants))

- Germany (Institut der Wirtschaftsprüfer in Deutschland (IDW) and the Wirtschaftsprüferkammer (WPK) (Chamber of Auditors))

- Japan Nihon Kouninkaikeishi Kyoukai)

- Mexico (Instituto Mexicano de Contadores Publicos (IMCP) (Mexican Institute of Public Accountants)) (removed from the board in 1987 due to non-payment of dues; resumed in 1995.)

- the Netherlands (Nederlands Instituut van Registeraccountants (NIVRA)

(Netherlands Institute of Registered Auditors))

- the United Kingdom and Ireland (counted as one) (Institute of Chartered Accountants in England and Wales (ICAEW), Institute of Chartered Accountants of Scotland (ICAS), Institute of Chartered Accountants in Ireland (ICAI), Association of Certified Accountants, Institute of Cost and Management Accountants, and the Institute of Municipal Treasurers and Accountants)

- the United States of America (American Institute of Certified Public Accountants (AICPA))

The Institute of Chartered Accountants of Nigeria became an associate member in 1976 and a member of the board from 1978 to 1987.

The National Council of Chartered Accountants (South Africa) became an associate member in 1974 and joined the board in 1978.

a. International Accounting Standards Committee
b. Upromise
c. Openda
d. Audit Command Language

41. _____ are cash, evidence of an ownership interest in an entity or deliver, cash or another financial instrument.

_____ can be categorized by form depending on whether they are cash instruments or derivative instruments:

- Cash instruments are _____ whose value is determined directly by markets. They can be divided into securities, which are readily transferable, and other cash instruments such as loans and deposits, where both borrower and lender have to agree on a transfer.
- Derivative instruments are _____ which derive their value from the value and characteristics of one or more underlying assets. They can be divided into exchange-traded derivatives and over-the-counter (OTC) derivatives.

Alternatively, _____ can be categorized by 'asset class' depending on whether they are equity based (reflecting ownership of the issuing entity) or debt based (reflecting a loan the investor has made to the issuing entity.) If it is debt, it can be further categorised into short term (less than one year) or long term.

Foreign Exchange instruments and transactions are neither debt nor equity based and belong in their own category.

a. Secondary market
b. Financial services
c. Cost of carry
d. Financial instruments

42. Straight-line depreciation is the simplest and most-often-used technique, in which the company estimates the _____ of the asset at the end of the period during which it will be used to generate revenues (useful life) and will expense a portion of original cost in equal increments over that period. The _____ is an estimate of the value of the asset at the time it will be sold or disposed of; it may be zero or even negative. _____ is scrap value, by another name.
a. Depreciation
b. Salvage value
c. Net profit
d. Fixed investment

43. _____ refers to any one of several methods by which a company, for 'financial accounting' and/or tax purposes, depreciates a fixed asset in such a way that the amount of depreciation taken each year is higher during the earlier years of an asset's life. For financial accounting purposes, _____ is generally used when an asset is expected to be much more productive during its early years, so that depreciation expense will more accurately represent how much of an asset's usefulness is being used up each year. For tax purposes, _____ provides a way of deferring corporate income taxes by reducing taxable income in current years, in exchange for increased taxable income in future years.

a. ABN Amro
b. A Random Walk Down Wall Street
c. Accelerated Depreciation
d. AAB

44. Depreciation methods that provide for a higher depreciation charge in the first year of an asset's life and gradually decreasing charges in subsequent years are called accelerated depreciation methods. This may be a more realistic reflection of an asset's actual expected benefit from the use of the asset: many assets are most useful when they are new. One popular accelerated method is the declining-balance method. Under this method the Book Value is multiplied by a fixed rate.

The most common rate used is double the straight-line rate. For this reason, this technique is referred to as the _____. To illustrate, suppose a business has an asset with $1,000 Original Cost, $100 Salvage Value, and 5 years useful life. First, calculate straight-line depreciation rate. Since the asset has 5 years useful life, the straight-line depreciation rate equals (100% / 5) 20% per year. With _____, as the name suggests, double that rate, or 40% depreciation rate is used.

a. Doctrine of the Proper Law
b. Double-declining-balance method
c. The Goodyear Tire ' Rubber Company
d. Database auditing

45. Accrual, in accounting, describes the accounting method known as _____, whereby revenues and expenses are recognized when they are accrued, i.e. accumulated (earned or incurred), regardless when the actual cash is received or paid out.

E.g. a company delivers a product to a customer who will pay for it 30 days later in the next fiscal year starting a week after the delivery. The company recognizes the proceeds as a revenue in its current income statement still for the fiscal year of the delivery, even though it will get paid in cash during the following accounting period.

a. A Random Walk Down Wall Street
b. Accrual basis
c. ABN Amro
d. AAB

Chapter 1. Financial Statements: An Overview

46. Two primary accounting methods, _____ and accrual basis, are used to calculate taxable income for U.S. federal income taxes. According to the Internal Revenue Code, a taxpayer may compute taxable income by:

1. the Cash receipts and disbursements method;
2. an accrual method;
3. any other method permitted by the chapter; or
4. any combination of the foregoing methods permitted under regulations prescribed by the Secretary.

As a general rule, a taxpayer must compute taxable income using the same accounting method he uses to compute income in keeping his books. Also, the taxpayer must maintain a consistent method of accounting from year to year. Should he change from the _____ to the accrual basis (or vice versa), he must notify and secure the consent of the Secretary.

a. 529 plan
b. 7-Eleven
c. Cash basis
d. 4-4-5 Calendar

47. _____ is a cornerstone of accrual accounting together with revenue recognition. They both determine the point, at which expenses and revenues are recognized. According to the principle, expenses are recognized when they are (1) incurred and (2) offset against recognized revenues, which were generated from those expenses (related on the cause-and-effect basis), no matter when cash is paid out.
a. Gross sales
b. Retained earnings
c. Matching principle
d. Pro forma

48. _____ is a specific term used in companies' financial reporting from the company-whole point of view. Because that use excludes the effects of changing ownership interest, an economic measure of _____ is necessary for financial analysis from the shareholders' point of view

_____ is defined by the Financial Accounting Standards Board, or FASB, as 'e;the change in equity [net assets] of a business enterprise during a period from transactions and other events and circumstances from nonowner sources. It includes all changes in equity during a period except those resulting from investments by owners and distributions to owners.'e;

_____ is the sum of net income and other items that must bypass the income statement because they have not been realized, including items like an unrealized holding gain or loss from available for sale securities and foreign currency translation gains or losses.

a. Comprehensive income
b. 7-Eleven
c. 4-4-5 Calendar
d. 529 plan

49. _____ is an accounting term used to reflect the portion of the book value of a business entity not directly attributable to its assets and liabilities; it normally arises only in case of an acquisition. It reflects the ability of the entity to make a higher profit than would be derived from selling the tangible assets. _____ is also known as an intangible asset.
   a. Consolidation
   b. Cost of goods sold
   c. Net profit
   d. Goodwill

50. _____ are defined as identifiable non-monetary assets that cannot be seen, touched or physically measured, which are created through time and/or effort and that are identifiable as a separate asset. There are two primary forms of intangibles - legal intangibles (such as trade secrets (e.g., customer lists), copyrights, patents, trademarks, and goodwill) and competitive intangibles (such as knowledge activities (know-how, knowledge), collaboration activities, leverage activities, and structural activities.) Legal intangibles generate legal property rights defensible in a court of law.
   a. Intangible assets
   b. ABN Amro
   c. A Random Walk Down Wall Street
   d. AAB

51. An _____ is a tax levied on the financial income of people, corporations, or other legal entities. Various _____ systems exist, with varying degrees of tax incidence. Income taxation can be progressive, proportional, or regressive.
   a. Income tax
   b. AAB
   c. A Random Walk Down Wall Street
   d. ABN Amro

52. In business, _____ is income that a company receives from its normal business activities, usually from the sale of goods and services to customers. Some companies also receive _____ from interest, dividends or royalties paid to them by other companies. _____ may refer to business income in general, or it may refer to the amount, in a monetary unit, received during a period of time, as in 'Last year, Company X had _____ of $32 million.'

In many countries, including the UK, _____ is referred to as turnover.

a. Bottom line
b. Furniture, Fixtures and Equipment
c. Revenue
d. Matching principle

53. _____ is the portion of income that is the subject of taxation according to the laws that determine what is income and the taxation rate for that income. Generally, _____ refers to an individual's (or corporation's) gross income, adjusted for various deductions allowable by statute. The main questions put by most individuals in any jurisdiction are 'what makes up my _____' and what tax rates should be applied such that I can work out my tax liability to the state.
a. 529 plan
b. 4-4-5 Calendar
c. 7-Eleven
d. Taxable income

54. The _____ is the current method of accelerated asset depreciation required by the United States income tax code. Under _____, all assets are divided into classes which dictate the number of years over which an asset's cost will be recovered.

Prior to the Accelerated Cost Recovery System (ACRS), most capital purchases were depreciated using a straight line technique, that allowed for the depreciation of the asset over its useful life.

a. 4-4-5 Calendar
b. Modified Accelerated Cost Recovery System
c. 7-Eleven
d. 529 plan

55. In economics, business, and accounting, a _____ is the value of money that has been used up to produce something, and hence is not available for use anymore. In business, the _____ may be one of acquisition, in which case the amount of money expended to acquire it is counted as _____. In this case, money is the input that is gone in order to acquire the thing.
a. Sliding scale fees
b. Cost
c. Marginal cost
d. Fixed costs

Chapter 1. Financial Statements: An Overview

56. _____, in accounting, refers to the overall reasonableness of reported earnings. It is an assessment criterion for how 'repeatable, controllable and bankable' a firm's earnings are, amongst other factors. It recognizes the fact that the economic impact of a given transaction will vary across firms as a function of their fundamental business characteristics, and has variously been defined as the degree to which earnings reflect underlying economic effects, are better estimates of cash flows, are conservative, or are predictable.
   a. Imprest system
   b. Installment Sales Method
   c. Unified Ledger Accounting
   d. Earnings quality

57. In business, investment, and accounting, the principle or convention of _____ has at least two meanings.

In investment and finance, it is a strategy which aims at long-term capital appreciation with low risk. It can be characterized as moderate or cautious and is the opposite of aggressive behavior.

   a. Barcampbank
   b. Conservatism
   c. Duration gap
   d. Debt-snowball method

58. In economic models, the _____ time frame assumes no fixed factors of production. Firms can enter or leave the marketplace, and the cost (and availability) of land, labor, raw materials, and capital goods can be assumed to vary. In contrast, in the short-run time frame, certain factors are assumed to be fixed, because there is not sufficient time for them to change.
   a. 4-4-5 Calendar
   b. Short-run
   c. 529 plan
   d. Long-run

59. The phrase _____ according to the Organization for Economic Co-operation and Development, refers to 'creative work undertaken on a systematic basis in order to increase the stock of knowledge, including knowledge of (hu)man, culture and society, and the use of this stock of knowledge to devise new applications'.

New product design and development is more than often a crucial factor in the survival of a company. In an industry that is fast changing, firms must continually revise their design and range of products. This is necessary due to continuous technology change and development as well as other competitors and the changing preference of customers.

a. 7-Eleven
b. 4-4-5 Calendar
c. 529 plan
d. Research and development

60. In finance, a _____ or accounting ratio is a ratio of two selected numerical values taken from an enterprise's financial statements. There are many standard ratios used to try to evaluate the overall financial condition of a corporation or other organization. They may be used by managers within a firm, by current and potential shareholders (owners) of a firm, and by a firm's creditors. Security analysts use these to compare the strengths and weaknesses in various companies.
a. Return on capital employed
b. Price/cash flow ratio
c. Sustainable growth rate
d. Financial ratio

Chapter 2. The Balance Sheet

1. In business and accounting, _____s are everything of value that is owned by a person or company. The balance sheet of a firm records the monetary value of the _____s owned by the firm. The two major _____ classes are tangible _____s and intangible _____s.
   a. Asset
   b. EBITDA
   c. Income
   d. Accounts payable

2. _____ is the field of accountancy concerned with the preparation of financial statements for decision makers, such as stockholders, suppliers, banks, employees, government agencies, owners, and other stakeholders. The fundamental need for _____ is to reduce principal-agent problem by measuring and monitoring agents' performance and reporting the results to interested users.

   _____ is used to prepare accounting information for people outside the organization or not involved in the day to day running of the company.

   a. 4-4-5 Calendar
   b. Financial Accounting
   c. 7-Eleven
   d. 529 plan

3. _____ are formal records of a business' financial activities.

   _____ provide an overview of a business' financial condition in both short and long term. There are four basic _____:

   1. **Balance sheet**: also referred to as statement of financial position or condition, reports on a company's assets, liabilities, and net equity as of a given point in time.
   2. **Income statement**: also referred to as Profit and Loss statement (or a 'P'L'), reports on a company's income, expenses, and profits over a period of time.
   3. **Statement of retained earnings**: explains the changes in a company's retained earnings over the reporting period.
   4. **Statement of cash flows**: reports on a company's cash flow activities, particularly its operating, investing and financing activities.

   a. Statement on Auditing Standards No. 70: Service Organizations
   b. Notes to the Financial Statements
   c. Statement of retained earnings
   d. Financial statements

Chapter 2. The Balance Sheet

4. _____ is a measure of the ability of a debtor to pay their debts as and when they fall due. It is usually expressed as a ratio or a percentage of current liabilities.

For a corporation with a published balance sheet there are various ratios used to calculate a measure of liquidity.

   a. Operating profit margin
   b. Accounting liquidity
   c. Operating leverage
   d. Invested capital

5. In financial accounting, a _____ or statement of financial position is a summary of a person's or organization's balances. Assets, liabilities and ownership equity are listed as of a specific date, such as the end of its financial year. A _____ is often described as a snapshot of a company's financial condition.

   a. Statement of retained earnings
   b. Statement on Auditing Standards No. 70: Service Organizations
   c. Financial statements
   d. Balance sheet

6. _____ is a form of corporation equity ownership represented in the securities. It is dangerous in comparison to preferred shares and some other investment options, in that in the event of bankruptcy, _____ investors receive their funds after preferred stockholders, bondholders, creditors, etc. On the other hand, common shares on average perform better than preferred shares or bonds over time.

   a. Stock split
   b. Common stock
   c. Stop-limit order
   d. Stock market bubble

7. _____ is a fee paid on borrowed assets. It is the price paid for the use of borrowed money , or, money earned by deposited funds . Assets that are sometimes lent with _____ include money, shares, consumer goods through hire purchase, major assets such as aircraft, and even entire factories in finance lease arrangements.

   a. AAB
   b. A Random Walk Down Wall Street
   c. Insolvency
   d. Interest

8. An _____ is the price a borrower pays for the use of money they do not own, and the return a lender receives for deferring the use of funds, by lending it to the borrower. _____s are normally expressed as a percentage rate over the period of one year.

_____s targets are also a vital tool of monetary policy and are used to control variables like investment, inflation, and unemployment.

a. AAB
b. Interest rate
c. ABN Amro
d. A Random Walk Down Wall Street

9. _____ in business is an accounting concept that refers to ownership of a company (subsidiary) that is less than 50% of outstanding shares. _____ belongs to other investors and is reported on the consolidated balance sheet of the owning company to reflect the claim on assets belonging to other, non-controlling shareholders. Also, _____ is reported on the consolidated income statement as a share of profit belonging to minority shareholders.

a. Fixed asset
b. Construction in Progress
c. Credit memo
d. Minority interest

10. _____ or amalgamation is the act of merging many things into one. In business, it often refers to the mergers or acquisitions of many smaller companies into much larger ones. The financial accounting term of _____ refers to the aggregated financial statements of a group company as consolidated account.

a. Write-off
b. Retained earnings
c. Cost of goods sold
d. Consolidation

11. A _____ (or financial year, or sometimes budget year) is a period used for calculating annual ('yearly') financial statements in businesses and other organizations. In many jurisdictions, regulatory laws regarding accounting and taxation require such reports once per twelve months, but do not require that the period reported on constitutes a calendar year (i.e., January through December.) _____s vary between businesses and countries.

a. Purchase ledger
b. Fiscal Year
c. Special journals
d. Matching principle

12. In finance, _____ refers to the way a corporation finances its assets through some combination of equity, debt, or hybrid securities. A firm's _____ is then the composition or 'structure' of its liabilities. For example, a firm that sells $20 billion in equity and $80 billion in debt is said to be 20% equity-financed and 80% debt-financed.

a. Rights issue
b. Capital structure
c. Book building
d. Market for corporate control

13. Depreciation methods that provide for a higher depreciation charge in the first year of an asset's life and gradually decreasing charges in subsequent years are called accelerated depreciation methods. This may be a more realistic reflection of an asset's actual expected benefit from the use of the asset: many assets are most useful when they are new. One popular accelerated method is the declining-balance method. Under this method the Book Value is multiplied by a fixed rate.

The most common rate used is double the straight-line rate. For this reason, this technique is referred to as the _____. To illustrate, suppose a business has an asset with $1,000 Original Cost, $100 Salvage Value, and 5 years useful life. First, calculate straight-line depreciation rate. Since the asset has 5 years useful life, the straight-line depreciation rate equals (100% / 5) 20% per year. With _____, as the name suggests, double that rate, or 40% depreciation rate is used.

a. Doctrine of the Proper Law
b. Double-declining-balance method
c. The Goodyear Tire ' Rubber Company
d. Database auditing

14. _____ is a term used in accounting, economics and finance to spread the cost of an asset over the span of several years.

In simple words we can say that _____ is the reduction in the value of an asset due to usage, passage of time, wear and tear, technological outdating or obsolescence, depletion or other such factors.

In accounting, _____ is a term used to describe any method of attributing the historical or purchase cost of an asset across its useful life, roughly corresponding to normal wear and tear.

a. Matching principle
b. Deferred financing costs
c. Bottom line
d. Depreciation

15. In accounting, a _____ is an asset on the balance sheet which is expected to be sold or otherwise used up in the near future, usually within one year, or one business cycle - whichever is longer. Typical _____s include cash, cash equivalents, accounts receivable, inventory, the portion of prepaid accounts which will be used within a year, and short-term investments.

On the balance sheet, assets will typically be classified into _____s and long-term assets.

   a. Current asset
   b. Historical cost
   c. Long-term liabilities
   d. Write-off

16. _____ is that which is owed; usually referencing assets owed, but the term can cover other obligations. In the case of assets, _____ is a means of using future purchasing power in the present before a summation has been earned. Some companies and corporations use _____ as a part of their overall corporate finance strategy.
   a. Cross-collateralization
   b. Credit cycle
   c. Partial Payment
   d. Debt

17. _____ are securities that can be easily converted into cash. Such securities will generally have highly liquid markets allowing the security to be sold at a reasonable price very quickly. This is a usual feature in real estate .
   a. Book entry
   b. Tracking stock
   c. Marketable
   d. Securities lending

18. _____ is a financial metric which represents operating liquidity available to a business. Along with fixed assets such as plant and equipment, _____ is considered a part of operating capital. It is calculated as current assets minus current liabilities.
   a. 529 plan
   b. 4-4-5 Calendar
   c. Working capital management
   d. Working capital

19. A _____ is a fungible, negotiable instrument representing financial value. They are broadly categorized into debt securities (such as banknotes, bonds and debentures), and equity securities; e.g., common stocks. The company or other entity issuing the _____ is called the issuer.

a. Book entry
b. Security
c. Tracking stock
d. Securities lending

20. _____ or accounting is the system of recording, verifying, and reporting of the value of assets, liabilities, income, and expenses in the books of account (ledger) to which debit and credit entries (recognizing transactions) are chronologically posted to record changes in value Such financial information is primarily used by lenders, managers, investors, tax authorities and other decision makers to make resource allocation decisions between and within companies, organizations, and public agencies. Accounting has been defined by the AICPA as ' The art of recording, classifying, and summarizing in a significant manner and in terms of money, transactions and events which are, in part at least, of financial character, and interpreting the results thereof.'

Financial accounting is one branch of accounting and historically has involved processes by which financial information about a business is recorded, classified, summarised, interpreted, and communicated; for public companies, this information is generally publicly-accessible.

a. A Random Walk Down Wall Street
b. AAB
c. ABN Amro
d. Accountancy

21. The role of the _____ is to issue accounting standards in the United Kingdom. It is recognised for that purpose under the Companies Act 1985. It took over the task of setting accounting standards from the Accounting Standards Committee (ASC) in 1990.
a. AAB
b. A Random Walk Down Wall Street
c. Accounting Standards Board
d. ABN Amro

22. In the global money market, _____ is an unsecured promissory note with a fixed maturity of one to 270 days. _____ is a money-market security issued (sold) by large banks and corporations to get money to meet short term debt obligations (for example, payroll), and is only backed by an issuing bank or corporation's promise to pay the face amount on the maturity date specified on the note. Since it is not backed by collateral, only firms with excellent credit ratings from a recognized rating agency will be able to sell their _____ at a reasonable price.

Chapter 2. The Balance Sheet

a. Financial distress
b. Book building
c. Commercial paper
d. Trade-off theory

23. _____ or First In, First Out, is an abstraction in ways of organizing and manipulation of data relative to time and prioritization. This expression describes the principle of a queue processing technique or servicing conflicting demands by ordering process by first-come, first-served (FCFS) behaviour: what comes in first is handled first, what comes in next waits until the first is finished, etc.

Thus it is analogous to the behaviour of persons queueing (or 'standing in line', in common American parlance), where the persons leave the queue in the order they arrive, or waiting one's turn at a traffic control signal.

a. Risk management
b. 4-4-5 Calendar
c. Penny stock
d. FIFO

24. The _____ is a private, not-for-profit organization whose primary purpose is to develop generally accepted accounting principles (GAAP) within the United States in the public's interest. The Securities and Exchange Commission (SEC) designated the _____ as the organization responsible for setting accounting standards for public companies in the U.S. It was created in 1973, replacing the Accounting Principles Board and the Committee on Accounting Procedure of the American Institute of Certified Public Accountants. The _____'s mission is 'to establish and improve standards of financial accounting and reporting for the guidance and education of the public, including issuers, auditors, and users of financial information.'

The _____ is not a governmental body.

a. Federal Deposit Insurance Corporation
b. KPMG
c. World Congress of Accountants
d. Financial Accounting Standards Board

25. _____ is a list for goods and materials held available in stock by a business. It is also used for a list of the contents of a household and for a list for testamentary purposes of the possessions of someone who has died. In accounting _____ is considered an asset.

a. ABN Amro
b. AAB
c. A Random Walk Down Wall Street
d. Inventory

26. _____ is a life of security. It may also refer to the final payment date of a loan or other financial instrument, at which point all remaining interest and principal is due to be paid.

1, 3, 6 months _____ band can be calculated by using 30-day per month periods.

a. Replacement cost
b. False billing
c. Primary market
d. Maturity

27. In accounting and finance, _____ is the portion of receivables that can no longer be collected, typically from accounts receivable or loans. _____ in accounting is considered an expense.

There are two methods to account for _____:

1. Direct write off method (Non - GAAP)

A receivable which is not considered collectible is charged directly to the income statement.

1. Allowance method (GAAP)

An estimate is made at the end of each fiscal year of the amount of _____. This is then accumulated in a provision which is then used to reduce specific receivable accounts as and when necessary.

a. Tax expense
b. 4-4-5 Calendar
c. 529 plan
d. Bad debt

28. _____, in bookkeeping, refers to assets, liabilities, income, and expenses recorded on individual pages of the so called book of final entry or ledger. Changes in _____ value are made by chronologically posting debit (DR) and credit (CR) entries to its page. Examples of _____s are cash, _____s receivable, mortgages, loans, land and buildings, common stock, sales, services provided, wages, and payroll overhead.

a. Option
b. Accretion
c. Alpha
d. Account

29. _____ is one of a series of accounting transactions dealing with the billing of customers who owe money to a person, company or organization for goods and services that have been provided to the customer. In most business entities this is typically done by generating an invoice and mailing or electronically delivering it to the customer, who in turn must pay it within an established timeframe called credit or payment terms.

An example of a common payment term is Net 30, meaning payment is due in the amount of the invoice 30 days from the date of invoice.

a. Accounting methods
b. Income
c. Impaired asset
d. Accounts receivable

30. In economics, business, and accounting, a _____ is the value of money that has been used up to produce something, and hence is not available for use anymore. In business, the _____ may be one of acquisition, in which case the amount of money expended to acquire it is counted as _____. In this case, money is the input that is gone in order to acquire the thing.
a. Sliding scale fees
b. Marginal cost
c. Fixed costs
d. Cost

31. In finance, _____ is the process of estimating the potential market value of a financial asset or liability. they can be done on assets (for example, investments in marketable securities such as stocks, options, business enterprises, or intangible assets such as patents and trademarks) or on liabilities (e.g., Bonds issued by a company.) _____s are required in many contexts including investment analysis, capital budgeting, merger and acquisition transactions, financial reporting, taxable events to determine the proper tax liability, and in litigation.
a. Margin
b. Share
c. Procter ' Gamble
d. Valuation

Chapter 2. The Balance Sheet

32. _____s are goods that have completed the manufacturing process but have not yet been sold or distributed to the end user.

Manufacturing has three classes of inventory:

1. Raw material
2. Work in process
3. _____s

A good purchased as a 'raw material' goes into the manufacture of a product. A good only partially completed during the manufacturing process is called 'work in process'. When the good is completed as to manufacturing but not yet sold or distributed to the end-user is called a '_____'.

a. 7-Eleven
b. 529 plan
c. 4-4-5 Calendar
d. Finished good

33. _____ is an acronym which stands for last in, first out. In computer science and queueing theory this refers to the way items stored in some types of data structures are processed. By definition, in a _____ structured linear list, elements can be added or taken off from only one end, called the 'top'.

a. 529 plan
b. 4-4-5 Calendar
c. 7-Eleven
d. LIFO

34. _____ is the discipline of identifying, monitoring and limiting risks. In some cases the acceptable risk may be near zero. Risks can come from accidents, natural causes and disasters as well as deliberate attacks from an adversary.

a. Risk Management
b. FIFO
c. Penny stock
d. 4-4-5 Calendar

35. _____, _____ includes the direct costs attributable to the production of the goods sold by a company. This amount includes the materials cost used in creating the goods along with the direct labor costs used to produce the good. It excludes indirect expenses such as distribution costs and sales force costs.

a. Deferred financing costs
b. Goodwill
c. Net profit
d. Cost of goods sold

36. _____ is the statutory title of qualified accountants in the United States who have passed the Uniform _____ Examination and have met additional state education and experience requirements for certification as a _____. In most U.S. states, only _____s who are licensed are able to provide to the public attestation (including auditing) opinions on financial statements. The exceptions to this rule are Arizona, Kansas, North Carolina and Ohio where, although the '_____' designation is restricted, the practice of auditing is not.
   a. Certified General Accountant
   b. Chartered Certified Accountant
   c. Chartered Accountant
   d. Certified Public Accountant

37. In accounting, _____ or *Carrying value* is the value of an asset according to its balance sheet account balance. For assets, the value is based on the original cost of the asset less any depreciation, amortization or impairment costs made against the asset. A company's _____ is its total assets minus intangible assets and liabilities.
   a. Book value
   b. Pro forma
   c. Retained earnings
   d. Current liabilities

38. _____ plant, and equipment, is a term used in accountancy for assets and property which cannot easily be converted into cash. This can be compared with current assets such as cash or bank accounts, which are described as liquid assets. In most cases, only tangible assets are referred to as fixed.
   a. Petty cash
   b. Percentage of Completion
   c. Remittance advice
   d. Fixed asset

Chapter 2. The Balance Sheet

39. _____ is the process of decreasing an amount over a period of time. The word comes from Middle English amortisen to kill, alienate in mortmain, from Anglo-French amorteser, alteration of amortir, from Vulgar Latin admortire to kill, from Latin ad- + mort-, mors death. Particular instances of the term include:

- _____ (business), the allocation of a lump sum amount to different time periods, particularly for loans and other forms of finance, including related interest or other finance charges.
    - _____ schedule, a table detailing each periodic payment on a loan (typically a mortgage), as generated by an _____ calculator.
    - Negative _____, an _____ schedule where the loan amount actually increases through not paying the full interest
- Amortized analysis, analyzing the execution cost of algorithms over a sequence of operations.
- _____ of capital expenditures of certain assets under accounting rules, particularly intangible assets, in a manner analogous to depreciation.
- _____ (tax law)

_____ is also used in the context of zoning regulations and describes the time in which a property owner has to relocate when the property's use constitutes a preexisting nonconforming use under zoning regulations.

- Depreciation

a. Option
b. Intrinsic value
c. Amortization
d. AT'T Inc.

40. _____ refers to any one of several methods by which a company, for 'financial accounting' and/or tax purposes, depreciates a fixed asset in such a way that the amount of depreciation taken each year is higher during the earlier years of an asset's life. For financial accounting purposes, _____ is generally used when an asset is expected to be much more productive during its early years, so that depreciation expense will more accurately represent how much of an asset's usefulness is being used up each year. For tax purposes, _____ provides a way of deferring corporate income taxes by reducing taxable income in current years, in exchange for increased taxable income in future years.
a. Accelerated Depreciation
b. ABN Amro
c. AAB
d. A Random Walk Down Wall Street

41. _____ is an accounting term used to reflect the portion of the book value of a business entity not directly attributable to its assets and liabilities; it normally arises only in case of an acquisition. It reflects the ability of the entity to make a higher profit than would be derived from selling the tangible assets. _____ is also known as an intangible asset.

a. Net profit
b. Cost of goods sold
c. Consolidation
d. Goodwill

42. _____ are defined as identifiable non-monetary assets that cannot be seen, touched or physically measured, which are created through time and/or effort and that are identifiable as a separate asset. There are two primary forms of intangibles - legal intangibles (such as trade secrets (e.g., customer lists), copyrights, patents, trademarks, and goodwill) and competitive intangibles (such as knowledge activities (know-how, knowledge), collaboration activities, leverage activities, and structural activities.) Legal intangibles generate legal property rights defensible in a court of law.
   a. Intangible assets
   b. A Random Walk Down Wall Street
   c. ABN Amro
   d. AAB

43. In economic models, the _____ time frame assumes no fixed factors of production. Firms can enter or leave the marketplace, and the cost (and availability) of land, labor, raw materials, and capital goods can be assumed to vary. In contrast, in the short-run time frame, certain factors are assumed to be fixed, because there is not sufficient time for them to change.
   a. 4-4-5 Calendar
   b. Short-run
   c. 529 plan
   d. Long-run

44. _____ is a file or account that contains money that a person or company owes to suppliers, but hasn't paid yet (a form of debt.) When you receive an invoice you add it to the file, and then you remove it when you pay. Thus, the A/P is a form of credit that suppliers offer to their purchasers by allowing them to pay for a product or service after it has already been received.
   a. Accounts payable
   b. Accrual
   c. Outstanding balance
   d. Earnings before interest, taxes, depreciation and amortization

45. In accounting, _____ are considered liabilities of the business that are to be settled in cash within the fiscal year or the operating cycle, whichever period is longer.

For example accounts payable for goods, services or supplies that were purchased for use in the operation of the business and payable within a normal period of time would be _____.

Bonds, mortgages and loans that are payable over a term exceeding one year would be fixed liabilities.

a. Current liabilities
b. Gross sales
c. Closing entries
d. Net income

46. In finance, a _____ or accounting ratio is a ratio of two selected numerical values taken from an enterprise's financial statements. There are many standard ratios used to try to evaluate the overall financial condition of a corporation or other organization. They may be used by managers within a firm, by current and potential shareholders (owners) of a firm, and by a firm's creditors. Security analysts use these to compare the strengths and weaknesses in various companies.

a. Return on capital employed
b. Sustainable growth rate
c. Price/cash flow ratio
d. Financial ratio

47. _____ are liabilities which have occurred, but have not been paid or logged under accounts payable during an accounting period; in other words, obligations for goods and services provided to a company for which invoices have not yet been received. Examples would include accrued wages payable, accrued sales tax payable, and accrued rent payable.

There are two general types of _____:

- Routine and recurring
- Infrequent or non-routine

a. Accounting methods
b. Outstanding balance
c. Adjusting entries
d. Accrued liabilities

48. The institution most often referenced by the word '_____' is a public or publicly traded _____, the shares of which are traded on a public stock exchange (e.g., the New York Stock Exchange or Nasdaq in the United States) where shares of stock of _____s are bought and sold by and to the general public. Most of the largest businesses in the world are publicly traded _____s. However, the majority of _____s are said to be closely held, privately held or close _____s, meaning that no ready market exists for the trading of shares.

Chapter 2. The Balance Sheet

a. Corporation
b. Depository Trust Company
c. Protect
d. Federal Home Loan Mortgage Corporation

49. _____, in accrual accounting, is any account where the asset or liability is not realized until a future date, e.g. annuities, charges, taxes, income, etc. The _____ item may be carried, dependent on type of deferral, as either an asset or liability. See also: accrual

_____ is also used in the university admissions process. It is the action by which a school rejects a student for early admission but still opts to review that student in the general admissions pool.

a. Deferred
b. Revenue
c. Net profit
d. Current asset

50. In financial accounting, the term _____ is most commonly used to describe any part of shareholders' equity, except for basic share capital. Sometimes, the term is used instead of the term provision; such a use, however, is inconsistent with the terminology suggested by International Accounting Standards Board. For more information about provisions, see provision (accounting.)

a. Closing entries
b. FIFO and LIFO accounting
c. Treasury stock
d. Reserve

51. _____ is the provision of resources (such as granting a loan) by one party to another party where that second party does not reimburse the first party immediately, thereby generating a debt, and instead arranges either to repay or return those resources (or material(s) of equal value) at a later date. The first party is called a creditor, also known as a lender, while the second party is called a debtor, also known as a borrower.

Movements of financial capital are normally dependent on either _____ or equity transfers.

a. Comparable
b. Clearing house
c. Credit
d. Warrant

Chapter 2. The Balance Sheet

52. In business, _____ is income that a company receives from its normal business activities, usually from the sale of goods and services to customers. Some companies also receive _____ from interest, dividends or royalties paid to them by other companies. _____ may refer to business income in general, or it may refer to the amount, in a monetary unit, received during a period of time, as in 'Last year, Company X had _____ of $32 million.'

In many countries, including the UK, _____ is referred to as turnover.

   a. Matching principle
   b. Bottom line
   c. Furniture, Fixtures and Equipment
   d. Revenue

53. _____, refers to consumption opportunity gained by an entity within a specified time frame, which is generally expressed in monetary terms. However, for households and individuals, '_____ is the sum of all the wages, salaries, profits, interests payments, rents and other forms of earnings received... in a given period of time.' For firms, _____ generally refers to net-profit: what remains of revenue after expenses have been subtracted.
   a. OIBDA
   b. Accrual
   c. Annual report
   d. Income

54. An _____ is a tax levied on the financial income of people, corporations, or other legal entities. Various _____ systems exist, with varying degrees of tax incidence. Income taxation can be progressive, proportional, or regressive.
   a. A Random Walk Down Wall Street
   b. AAB
   c. ABN Amro
   d. Income tax

55. _____ is the portion of income that is the subject of taxation according to the laws that determine what is income and the taxation rate for that income. Generally, _____ refers to an individual's (or corporation's) gross income, adjusted for various deductions allowable by statute. The main questions put by most individuals in any jurisdiction are 'what makes up my _____' and what tax rates should be applied such that I can work out my tax liability to the state.
   a. Taxable income
   b. 4-4-5 Calendar
   c. 529 plan
   d. 7-Eleven

38   Chapter 2. The Balance Sheet

56. _____ are liabilities with a future benefit over one year, such as notes payable that mature greater than one year.

In accounting, the _____ are shown on the right wing of the balance-sheet representing the sources of funds, which are generally bounded in form of capital assets.

Examples of _____ are debentures, mortgage loans and other bank loans (note: not all bank loans are long term as not all are paid over a period greater than a year, the example is bridging loan.)

    a. Bottom line
    b. Deferred income
    c. Matching principle
    d. Long-term Liabilities

57. The term _____ has three unrelated technical definitions, and is also used in a variety of non-technical ways.

- In financial economics, it refers to any asset used to make money, as opposed to assets used for personal enjoyment or consumption. This is an important distinction because two people can disagree sharply about the value of personal assets, one person might think a sports car is more valuable than a pickup truck, another person might have the opposite taste. But if an asset is held for the purpose of making money, taste has nothing to do with it, only differences of opinion about how much money the asset will produce. With the further assumption that people agree on the probability distribution of future cash flows, it is possible to have an objective _____ pricing model. Even without the assumption of agreement, it is possible to set rational limits on _____ value.
- In governmental accounting, it is defined as any asset used in operations with an initial useful life extending beyond one reporting period. Generally, government managers have a 'stewardship' duty to maintain _____s under their control. See International Public Sector Accounting Standards for details.
- In US tax accounting, it is defined as any property other than a list of exceptions. The main exceptions are anything held for sale, and any real estate or depreciable property used in business. Almost everything you own and use for personal purposes, pleasure or investment is a _____. If something is a _____ for tax purposes, gains or losses on sale or disposition are capital gains or capital losses. For individuals, however, capital losses on property held for personal use are generally not deductible. See the IRS publication Tax Facts about Capital Gains and Losses for details.

A well-known financial accounting textbook advises that the term be avoided except in tax accounting because it is used in so many different senses, not all of them well-defined. For example it is often used as a synonym for fixed assets or for investments in securities.

A common non-technical usage occurs when people ask that employees or the environment or something else be treated as a _____.

a. Political risk
b. Solvency
c. Capital asset
d. Settlement date

58. An _____ is a lease whose term is short compared to the useful life of the asset or piece of equipment (an airliner, a ship etc.) being leased. An _____ is commonly used to acquire equipment on a relatively short-term basis.
   a. ABN Amro
   b. AAB
   c. A Random Walk Down Wall Street
   d. Operating lease

59. _____ or financing is to provide capital (funds), which means money for a project, a person, a business or any other private or public institutions.

Those funds can be allocated for either short term or long term purposes. The health fund is a new way of _____ private healthcare centers.

   a. Synthetic CDO
   b. Proxy fight
   c. Product life cycle
   d. Funding

60. _____ is typically a higher ranking stock than voting shares, and its terms are negotiated between the corporation and the investor.

_____ usually carry no voting rights, but may carry superior priority over common stock in the payment of dividends and upon liquidation. _____ may carry a dividend that is paid out prior to any dividends to common stock holders.

   a. Second lien loan
   b. Follow-on offering
   c. Trade-off theory
   d. Preferred stock

61. _____, in finance and accounting, means stated value or face value. From this comes the expressions at par (at the _____), over par (over _____) and under par (under _____.)

The term '_____' has several meanings depending on context and geography.

a. Par value
b. FIDC
c. Sinking fund
d. Global Squeeze

62. In accounting, _____ refers to the portion of net income which is retained by the corporation rather than distributed to its owners as dividends. Similarly, if the corporation makes a loss, then that loss is retained and called variously retained losses, accumulated losses or accumulated deficit. _____ and losses are cumulative from year to year with losses offsetting earnings.
a. Historical cost
b. Retained earnings
c. Generally Accepted Accounting Principles
d. Matching principle

63. _____ are those dividends paid out in form of additional stock shares of the issuing corporation or other corporation They are usually issued in proportion to shares owned (for example for every 100 shares of stock owned, 5% stock dividend will yield 5 extra shares). If this payment involves the issue of new shares, this is very similar to a stock split in that it increases the total number of shares while lowering the price of each share and does not change the market capitalization or the total value of the shares held
a. Stock or scrip dividends
b. The Hong Kong Securities Institute
c. Database auditing
d. Time-based currency

64. A _____ or reacquired stock is stock which is bought back by the issuing company, reducing the amount of outstanding stock on the open market ('open market' including insiders' holdings.)

Stock repurchases are often used as a tax-efficient method to put cash into shareholders' hands, rather than pay dividends. Sometimes, companies do this when they feel that their stock is undervalued on the open market.

a. Treasury stock
b. Current asset
c. Generally Accepted Accounting Principles
d. Trial balance

Chapter 2. The Balance Sheet

65. A _____ is a payment made by a corporation to its shareholder members. When a corporation earns a profit or surplus, that money can be put to two uses: it can either be re-invested in the business (called retained earnings), or it can be paid to the shareholders as a _____. Many corporations retain a portion of their earnings and pay the remainder as a _____.

   a. Dividend yield
   b. Dividend puzzle
   c. Special dividend
   d. Dividend

66. _____ is a specific term used in companies' financial reporting from the company-whole point of view. Because that use excludes the effects of changing ownership interest, an economic measure of _____ is necessary for financial analysis from the shareholders' point of view

   _____ is defined by the Financial Accounting Standards Board, or FASB, as 'e;the change in equity [net assets] of a business enterprise during a period from transactions and other events and circumstances from nonowner sources. It includes all changes in equity during a period except those resulting from investments by owners and distributions to owners.'e;

   _____ is the sum of net income and other items that must bypass the income statement because they have not been realized, including items like an unrealized holding gain or loss from available for sale securities and foreign currency translation gains or losses.

   a. 4-4-5 Calendar
   b. 529 plan
   c. 7-Eleven
   d. Comprehensive income

67. _____ means regulating, adapting or settling in a variety of contexts:

   In commercial law, _____ means the settlement of a loss incurred on insured goods. The calculation of the amounts of compensation to be paid by or to the several interests is a complicated matter. It involves much detail and arithmetic, and requires a full and accurate knowledge of the principles of the subject.

   a. Equity method
   b. Asset recovery
   c. Intelligent investor
   d. Adjustment

Chapter 3. Income Statement and Statement of Stockholders Equity

1. _____ is the field of accountancy concerned with the preparation of financial statements for decision makers, such as stockholders, suppliers, banks, employees, government agencies, owners, and other stakeholders. The fundamental need for _____ is to reduce principal-agent problem by measuring and monitoring agents' performance and reporting the results to interested users.

_____ is used to prepare accounting information for people outside the organization or not involved in the day to day running of the company.

   a. 529 plan
   b. 7-Eleven
   c. Financial Accounting
   d. 4-4-5 Calendar

2. _____ are formal records of a business' financial activities.

_____ provide an overview of a business' financial condition in both short and long term. There are four basic _____:

   1. **Balance sheet**: also referred to as statement of financial position or condition, reports on a company's assets, liabilities, and net equity as of a given point in time.
   2. **Income statement**: also referred to as Profit and Loss statement (or a 'P'L'), reports on a company's income, expenses, and profits over a period of time.
   3. **Statement of retained earnings**: explains the changes in a company's retained earnings over the reporting period.
   4. **Statement of cash flows**: reports on a company's cash flow activities, particularly its operating, investing and financing activities.

   a. Statement of retained earnings
   b. Notes to the Financial Statements
   c. Financial statements
   d. Statement on Auditing Standards No. 70: Service Organizations

3. _____, refers to consumption opportunity gained by an entity within a specified time frame, which is generally expressed in monetary terms. However, for households and individuals, '_____ is the sum of all the wages, salaries, profits, interests payments, rents and other forms of earnings received... in a given period of time.' For firms, _____ generally refers to net-profit: what remains of revenue after expenses have been subtracted.
   a. OIBDA
   b. Accrual
   c. Annual report
   d. Income

Chapter 3. Income Statement and Statement of Stockholders Equity 43

4. An _____ is a financial statement for companies that indicates how Revenue is transformed into net income The purpose of the _____ is to show managers and investors whether the company made or lost money during the period being reported.

The important thing to remember about an _____ is that it represents a period of time.

 a. ABN Amro
 b. AAB
 c. A Random Walk Down Wall Street
 d. Income statement

5. The _____ is the current method of accelerated asset depreciation required by the United States income tax code. Under _____, all assets are divided into classes which dictate the number of years over which an asset's cost will be recovered.

Prior to the Accelerated Cost Recovery System (ACRS), most capital purchases were depreciated using a straight line technique, that allowed for the depreciation of the asset over its useful life.

 a. Modified Accelerated Cost Recovery System
 b. 529 plan
 c. 7-Eleven
 d. 4-4-5 Calendar

6. Two primary accounting methods, _____ and accrual basis, are used to calculate taxable income for U.S. federal income taxes. According to the Internal Revenue Code, a taxpayer may compute taxable income by:

 1. the Cash receipts and disbursements method;
 2. an accrual method;
 3. any other method permitted by the chapter; or
 4. any combination of the foregoing methods permitted under regulations prescribed by the Secretary.

As a general rule, a taxpayer must compute taxable income using the same accounting method he uses to compute income in keeping his books. Also, the taxpayer must maintain a consistent method of accounting from year to year. Should he change from the _____ to the accrual basis (or vice versa), he must notify and secure the consent of the Secretary.

 a. 4-4-5 Calendar
 b. Cash basis
 c. 529 plan
 d. 7-Eleven

Chapter 3. Income Statement and Statement of Stockholders Equity

7. _____ is the balance of the amounts of cash being received and paid by a business during a defined period of time, sometimes tied to a specific project. Measurement of _____ can be used

- to evaluate the state or performance of a business or project.
- to determine problems with liquidity. Being profitable does not necessarily mean being liquid. A company can fail because of a shortage of cash, even while profitable.
- to generate project rate of returns. The time of _____s into and out of projects are used as inputs to financial models such as internal rate of return, and net present value.
- to examine income or growth of a business when it is believed that accrual accounting concepts do not represent economic realities. Alternately, _____ can be used to 'validate' the net income generated by accrual accounting.

_____ as a generic term may be used differently depending on context, and certain _____ definitions may be adapted by analysts and users for their own uses. Common terms include operating _____ and free _____.

_____s can be classified into:

1. Operational _____s: Cash received or expended as a result of the company's core business activities.
2. Investment _____s: Cash received or expended through capital expenditure, investments or acquisitions.
3. Financing _____s: Cash received or expended as a result of financial activities, such as interests and dividends.

All three together - the net _____ - are necessary to reconcile the beginning cash balance to the ending cash balance. Loan draw downs or equity injections, that is just shifting of capital but no expenditure as such, are not considered in the net _____.

a. Cash flow
b. Real option
c. Corporate finance
d. Shareholder value

8. _____ is a specific term used in companies' financial reporting from the company-whole point of view. Because that use excludes the effects of changing ownership interest, an economic measure of _____ is necessary for financial analysis from the shareholders' point of view

_____ is defined by the Financial Accounting Standards Board, or FASB, as 'e;the change in equity [net assets] of a business enterprise during a period from transactions and other events and circumstances from nonowner sources. It includes all changes in equity during a period except those resulting from investments by owners and distributions to owners.'e;

_____ is the sum of net income and other items that must bypass the income statement because they have not been realized, including items like an unrealized holding gain or loss from available for sale securities and foreign currency translation gains or losses.

   a. 4-4-5 Calendar
   b. 529 plan
   c. Comprehensive income
   d. 7-Eleven

9. In economics, business, and accounting, a _____ is the value of money that has been used up to produce something, and hence is not available for use anymore. In business, the _____ may be one of acquisition, in which case the amount of money expended to acquire it is counted as _____. In this case, money is the input that is gone in order to acquire the thing.
   a. Fixed costs
   b. Sliding scale fees
   c. Marginal cost
   d. Cost

10. _____, _____ includes the direct costs attributable to the production of the goods sold by a company. This amount includes the materials cost used in creating the goods along with the direct labor costs used to produce the good. It excludes indirect expenses such as distribution costs and sales force costs.
    a. Goodwill
    b. Net profit
    c. Cost of goods sold
    d. Deferred financing costs

11. The role of the _____ is to issue accounting standards in the United Kingdom. It is recognised for that purpose under the Companies Act 1985. It took over the task of setting accounting standards from the Accounting Standards Committee (ASC) in 1990.
    a. Accounting Standards Board
    b. A Random Walk Down Wall Street
    c. ABN Amro
    d. AAB

Chapter 3. Income Statement and Statement of Stockholders Equity

12. _____ or First In, First Out, is an abstraction in ways of organizing and manipulation of data relative to time and prioritization. This expression describes the principle of a queue processing technique or servicing conflicting demands by ordering process by first-come, first-served (FCFS) behaviour: what comes in first is handled first, what comes in next waits until the first is finished, etc.

Thus it is analogous to the behaviour of persons queueing (or 'standing in line', in common American parlance), where the persons leave the queue in the order they arrive, or waiting one's turn at a traffic control signal.

   a. Risk management
   b. 4-4-5 Calendar
   c. Penny stock
   d. FIFO

13. The _____ is a private, not-for-profit organization whose primary purpose is to develop generally accepted accounting principles (GAAP) within the United States in the public's interest. The Securities and Exchange Commission (SEC) designated the _____ as the organization responsible for setting accounting standards for public companies in the U.S. It was created in 1973, replacing the Accounting Principles Board and the Committee on Accounting Procedure of the American Institute of Certified Public Accountants. The _____'s mission is 'to establish and improve standards of financial accounting and reporting for the guidance and education of the public, including issuers, auditors, and users of financial information.'

The _____ is not a governmental body.

   a. World Congress of Accountants
   b. KPMG
   c. Financial Accounting Standards Board
   d. Federal Deposit Insurance Corporation

14. _____ is a list for goods and materials held available in stock by a business. It is also used for a list of the contents of a household and for a list for testamentary purposes of the possessions of someone who has died. In accounting _____ is considered an asset.
   a. A Random Walk Down Wall Street
   b. AAB
   c. ABN Amro
   d. Inventory

Chapter 3. Income Statement and Statement of Stockholders Equity 47

15. Depreciation methods that provide for a higher depreciation charge in the first year of an asset's life and gradually decreasing charges in subsequent years are called accelerated depreciation methods. This may be a more realistic reflection of an asset's actual expected benefit from the use of the asset: many assets are most useful when they are new. One popular accelerated method is the declining-balance method. Under this method the Book Value is multiplied by a fixed rate.

The most common rate used is double the straight-line rate. For this reason, this technique is referred to as the _____. To illustrate, suppose a business has an asset with $1,000 Original Cost, $100 Salvage Value, and 5 years useful life. First, calculate straight-line depreciation rate. Since the asset has 5 years useful life, the straight-line depreciation rate equals (100% / 5) 20% per year. With _____, as the name suggests, double that rate, or 40% depreciation rate is used.

a. Double-declining-balance method
b. Doctrine of the Proper Law
c. The Goodyear Tire ' Rubber Company
d. Database auditing

16. _____ is a term used in accounting, economics and finance to spread the cost of an asset over the span of several years.

In simple words we can say that _____ is the reduction in the value of an asset due to usage, passage of time, wear and tear, technological outdating or obsolescence, depletion or other such factors.

In accounting, _____ is a term used to describe any method of attributing the historical or purchase cost of an asset across its useful life, roughly corresponding to normal wear and tear.

a. Deferred financing costs
b. Bottom line
c. Depreciation
d. Matching principle

17. A _____ is a measure of the average price of consumer goods and services purchased by households. The _____ can be used to index (i.e., adjust for the effects of inflation) wages, salaries, pensions, or regulated or contracted prices. The _____ is, along with the population census and the National Income and Product Accounts, one of the most closely watched national economic statistics.

a. Consumer Price Index
b. 529 plan
c. 4-4-5 Calendar
d. Divisia index

18. _____ is an acronym which stands for last in, first out. In computer science and queueing theory this refers to the way items stored in some types of data structures are processed. By definition, in a _____ structured linear list, elements can be added or taken off from only one end, called the 'top'.

   a. 529 plan
   b. LIFO
   c. 4-4-5 Calendar
   d. 7-Eleven

19. In bookkeeping, accounting, and finance, _____ are operating revenues earned by a company when it sells its products. Revenue _____ are reported directly on the income statement as Sales or _____.

In financial ratios that use income statement sales values, 'sales' refers to _____, not gross sales.

   a. Depletion
   b. Journal entry
   c. Closing entries
   d. Net sales

20. An _____, operating expenditure, operational expense, operational expenditure or OPEX is an on-going cost for running a product, business, or system. Its counterpart, a capital expenditure (CAPEX), is the cost of developing or providing non-consumable parts for the product or system. For example, the purchase of a photocopier is the CAPEX, and the annual paper and toner cost is the OPEX.

   a. AAB
   b. ABN Amro
   c. A Random Walk Down Wall Street
   d. Operating expense

21. A _____ is a normalized average (typically a weighted average) of prices for a given class of goods or services in a given region, during a given interval of time. It is a statistic designed to help to compare how these prices, taken as a whole, differ between time periods or geographical locations.

   a. Price discrimination
   b. Transfer pricing
   c. Discounts and allowances
   d. Price Index

Chapter 3. Income Statement and Statement of Stockholders Equity

22. In finance, _____ is the process of estimating the potential market value of a financial asset or liability. they can be done on assets (for example, investments in marketable securities such as stocks, options, business enterprises, or intangible assets such as patents and trademarks) or on liabilities (e.g., Bonds issued by a company.) _____s are required in many contexts including investment analysis, capital budgeting, merger and acquisition transactions, financial reporting, taxable events to determine the proper tax liability, and in litigation.

   a. Valuation
   b. Share
   c. Margin
   d. Procter ' Gamble

23. _____, Gross profit margin or Gross Profit Rate can be defined as the amount of contribution to the business enterprise, after paying for direct-fixed and direct-variable unit costs, required to cover overheads (fixed commitments) and provide a buffer for unknown items. It expresses the relationship between gross profit and sales revenue.

It can be expressed in absolute terms:

Gross Profit = Revenue >− Cost of Goods Sold

or as the ratio of gross profit to sales revenue, usually in the form of a percentage:

_____ Percentage = (Revenue-Cost of Goods Sold)/Revenue

Cost of goods sold includes variable costs and fixed costs directly linked to the product, such as material and labor. It does not include indirect fixed costs like office expenses, rent, administrative costs, etc.

   a. Gross margin
   b. Net profit margin
   c. 4-4-5 Calendar
   d. Profit margin

24. In accounting, _____ or sales profit is the difference between revenue and the cost of making a product or providing a service, before deducting overhead, payroll, taxation, and interest payments. Note that this is different than operating profit.

Net sales are calculated:

   Net sales = Sales - Sales returns and allowances

_____ is found by deducting the cost of goods sold:

   _____ = Net sales - Cost of goods sold

_____ should not be confused with net income:

   Net income = _____ - Total operating expenses

Cost of goods sold is calculated differently for merchandising business than for a manufacturer.

a. Gross income
b. Cash flow
c. Gross profit
d. Real option

25. _____ is a financial ratio used to assess the profitability of a firm's core activities, excluding fixed costs.

The general calculation is

$$\text{Gross profit margin} = \frac{\text{Revenue} - \text{Cost of Sales}}{\text{Revenue}}$$

The _____ is related to the net profit margin, which assesses the profitability of an organization after including fixed costs.

Indicates the relationship between net sales revenue and the cost of goods sold.

a. Gross profit margin
b. Second lien loan
c. Tender offer
d. Gross profit

26. _____ is the discipline of identifying, monitoring and limiting risks. In some cases the acceptable risk may be near zero. Risks can come from accidents, natural causes and disasters as well as deliberate attacks from an adversary.
a. 4-4-5 Calendar
b. Penny stock
c. FIFO
d. Risk Management

Chapter 3. Income Statement and Statement of Stockholders Equity

27. In finance, a _____ is collateral that the holder of a position in securities, options, or futures contracts has to deposit to cover the credit risk of his counterparty (most often his broker.) This risk can arise if the holder has done any of the following:

- borrowed cash from the counterparty to buy securities or options,
- sold securities or options short, or
- entered into a futures contract.

The collateral can be in the form of cash or securities, and it is deposited in a _____ account. On U.S. futures exchanges, '_____' was formally called performance bond.

_____ buying is buying securities with cash borrowed from a broker, using other securities as collateral.

a. Procter ' Gamble
b. Share
c. Credit
d. Margin

28. _____ is the difference between price and the costs of bringing to market whatever it is that is accounted as an enterprise (whether by harvest, extraction, manufacture, or purchase) in terms of the component costs of delivered goods and/or services and any operating or other expenses.

A key difficulty in measuring profit is in defining costs. Pure economic monetary profits can be zero or negative even in competitive equilibrium when accounted monetized costs exceed monetized price.

a. AAB
b. A Random Walk Down Wall Street
c. Economic profit
d. Accounting profit

29. _____, Net Margin, Net _____ or Net Profit Ratio all refer to a measure of profitability. It is calculated using a formula and written as a percentage or a number.

$$\text{Net profit margin} = \frac{\text{Net profit after taxes}}{\text{Net Sales}}$$

The _____ is mostly used for internal comparison.

a. 4-4-5 Calendar
b. Profit maximization
c. Profit margin
d. Net profit margin

30. In business and accounting, _____s are everything of value that is owned by a person or company. The balance sheet of a firm records the monetary value of the _____s owned by the firm. The two major _____ classes are tangible _____s and intangible _____s.
a. Asset
b. Income
c. EBITDA
d. Accounts payable

31. _____ plant, and equipment, is a term used in accountancy for assets and property which cannot easily be converted into cash. This can be compared with current assets such as cash or bank accounts, which are described as liquid assets. In most cases, only tangible assets are referred to as fixed.
a. Petty cash
b. Remittance advice
c. Fixed asset
d. Percentage of Completion

32. _____ is the process of decreasing an amount over a period of time. The word comes from Middle English amortisen to kill, alienate in mortmain, from Anglo-French amorteser, alteration of amortir, from Vulgar Latin admortire to kill, from Latin ad- + mort-, mors death. Particular instances of the term include:

- _____ (business), the allocation of a lump sum amount to different time periods, particularly for loans and other forms of finance, including related interest or other finance charges.
    - _____ schedule, a table detailing each periodic payment on a loan (typically a mortgage), as generated by an _____ calculator.
    - Negative _____, an _____ schedule where the loan amount actually increases through not paying the full interest
- Amortized analysis, analyzing the execution cost of algorithms over a sequence of operations.
- _____ of capital expenditures of certain assets under accounting rules, particularly intangible assets, in a manner analogous to depreciation.
- _____ (tax law)

Chapter 3. Income Statement and Statement of Stockholders Equity

_____ is also used in the context of zoning regulations and describes the time in which a property owner has to relocate when the property's use constitutes a preexisting nonconforming use under zoning regulations.

- Depreciation

a. Amortization
b. Option
c. AT'T Inc.
d. Intrinsic value

33. An _____ is a lease whose term is short compared to the useful life of the asset or piece of equipment (an airliner, a ship etc.) being leased. An _____ is commonly used to acquire equipment on a relatively short-term basis.
   a. ABN Amro
   b. Operating lease
   c. A Random Walk Down Wall Street
   d. AAB

34. Leasing is a process by which a firm can obtain the use of a certain fixed assets for which it must pay a series of contractual, periodic, tax deductable payments. The lessee is the receiver of the services or the assets under the lease contract and the lessor is the owner of the assets. The relationship between the tenant and the landlord is called a _____, and can be for a fixed or an indefinite period of time (called the term of the lease.)
   a. Tenancy
   b. REIT
   c. Real Estate Investment Trust
   d. Real estate investing

35. _____ is an accounting concept used most often in mining, timber, petroluem, or other similar industries. The _____ deduction allows an owner or operator to account for the reduction of a product's reserves. _____ is similar to depreciation in that, it is a cost recovery system for accounting and tax reporting.
   a. Net profit
   b. Deferred income
   c. Depletion
   d. Current liabilities

Chapter 3. Income Statement and Statement of Stockholders Equity

36. _____ is a fee paid on borrowed assets. It is the price paid for the use of borrowed money, or, money earned by deposited funds. Assets that are sometimes lent with _____ include money, shares, consumer goods through hire purchase, major assets such as aircraft, and even entire factories in finance lease arrangements.
   a. A Random Walk Down Wall Street
   b. AAB
   c. Insolvency
   d. Interest

37. _____ relates to the cost of borrowing money. It is the price that a lender charges a borrower for the use of the lender's money. _____ is different from OPEX and CAPEX, for it relates to the capital structure of a company.
   a. Interest expense
   b. AAB
   c. A Random Walk Down Wall Street
   d. ABN Amro

38. _____ is a measure of a company's earning power from ongoing operations, equal to earnings before the deduction of interest payments and income taxes.

To accountants, economic profit, or EP, is a single-period metric to determine the value created by a company in one period - usually a year. It is the net profit after tax less the equity charge, a risk-weighted cost of capital.

   a. Operating profit
   b. AAB
   c. Economic profit
   d. A Random Walk Down Wall Street

39. In business, operating margin, operating income margin, _____ or return on sales (ROS) is the ratio of operating income (operating profit in the UK) divided by net sales, usually presented in percent.

(Relevant figures in italics)

It is a measurement of what proportion of a company's revenue is left over, before taxes and other indirect costs (such as rent, bonus, interest, etc.), after paying for variable costs of production as wages, raw materials, etc. A good operating margin is needed for a company to be able to pay for its fixed costs, such as interest on debt.

Chapter 3. Income Statement and Statement of Stockholders Equity

a. Operating leverage
b. Operating profit margin
c. Average rate of return
d. Interest coverage ratio

40. The phrase _____ according to the Organization for Economic Co-operation and Development, refers to 'creative work undertaken on a systematic basis in order to increase the stock of knowledge, including knowledge of (hu)man, culture and society, and the use of this stock of knowledge to devise new applications'.

New product design and development is more than often a crucial factor in the survival of a company. In an industry that is fast changing, firms must continually revise their design and range of products. This is necessary due to continuous technology change and development as well as other competitors and the changing preference of customers.

a. 7-Eleven
b. 4-4-5 Calendar
c. 529 plan
d. Research and development

41. The _____ is the former authoritative body of the American Institute of Certified Public Accountants (AICPA.) It was created by the American Institute of Certified Public Accountants in 1959 and issued pronouncements on accounting principles until 1973, when it was replaced by the Financial Accounting Standards Board (FASB.)

The _____ was disbanded in the hopes that the smaller, fully-independent FASB could more effectively create accounting standards.

a. American Accounting Association
b. Upromise
c. Accounting Principles Board
d. Openda

42. A _____ is a payment made by a corporation to its shareholder members. When a corporation earns a profit or surplus, that money can be put to two uses: it can either be re-invested in the business (called retained earnings), or it can be paid to the shareholders as a _____. Many corporations retain a portion of their earnings and pay the remainder as a _____.

a. Dividend yield
b. Dividend puzzle
c. Dividend
d. Special dividend

43. _____ in accounting is the process of treating equity investments, usually 20-50%, in associate companies. The investor keeps such equities as an asset. Proportional share of associate company's net income increases the investment, and proportional payment of dividends decreases it.
a. Earnings growth
b. Ownership equity
c. Annuity
d. Equity method

44. _____ is that which is owed; usually referencing assets owed, but the term can cover other obligations. In the case of assets, _____ is a means of using future purchasing power in the present before a summation has been earned. Some companies and corporations use _____ as a part of their overall corporate finance strategy.
a. Partial Payment
b. Debt
c. Credit cycle
d. Cross-collateralization

45. A _____ is a fungible, negotiable instrument representing financial value. They are broadly categorized into debt securities (such as banknotes, bonds and debentures), and equity securities; e.g., common stocks. The company or other entity issuing the _____ is called the issuer.
a. Book entry
b. Tracking stock
c. Security
d. Securities lending

46. A _____, in business matters, is an entity that is controlled by a bigger and more powerful entity. The controlled entity is called a company, corporation, or limited liability company, and the controlling entity is called its parent (or the parent company.) The reason for this distinction is that a lone company cannot be a _____ of any organization; only an entity representing a legal fiction as a separate entity can be a _____.

Chapter 3. Income Statement and Statement of Stockholders Equity

a. 4-4-5 Calendar
b. Joint stock company
c. 529 plan
d. Subsidiary

47. _____, in accounting, refers to the overall reasonableness of reported earnings. It is an assessment criterion for how 'repeatable, controllable and bankable' a firm's earnings are, amongst other factors. It recognizes the fact that the economic impact of a given transaction will vary across firms as a function of their fundamental business characteristics , and has variously been defined as the degree to which earnings reflect underlying economic effects, are better estimates of cash flows, are conservative, or are predictable.

a. Earnings quality
b. Imprest system
c. Installment Sales Method
d. Unified Ledger Accounting

48. An _____ is a tax levied on the financial income of people, corporations, or other legal entities. Various _____ systems exist, with varying degrees of tax incidence. Income taxation can be progressive, proportional, or regressive.

a. ABN Amro
b. A Random Walk Down Wall Street
c. AAB
d. Income tax

49. _____ is a form of corporation equity ownership represented in the securities. It is dangerous in comparison to preferred shares and some other investment options, in that in the event of bankruptcy, _____ investors receive their funds after preferred stockholders, bondholders, creditors, etc. On the other hand, common shares on average perform better than preferred shares or bonds over time.

a. Stock market bubble
b. Stock split
c. Stop-limit order
d. Common stock

50. In finance, a _____ is a type of bond that can be converted into shares of stock in the issuing company, usually at some pre-announced ratio. It is a hybrid security with debt- and equity-like features. Although it typically has a low coupon rate, the holder is compensated with the ability to convert the bond to common stock, usually at a substantial discount to the stock's market value.

Chapter 3. Income Statement and Statement of Stockholders Equity

a. Convertible bond
b. Corporate bond
c. Bond fund
d. Gilts

51. _____ is a company's earnings per share (EPS) calculated using fully diluted shares outstanding (i.e. including the impact of stock option grants and convertible bonds.) Diluted EPS indicates a 'worst case' scenario, one in which everyone who could have received stock without purchasing it directly for the full market value did so.

To find diluted EPS, basic EPS is calculated for each of the categories on the income statement first.

a. Net assets
b. Price/cash flow ratio
c. Financial ratio
d. Diluted earnings per share

52. In financial and business accounting, _____ is a measure of a firm's profitability that excludes interest and income tax expenses.

EBIT = Operating Revenue - Operating Expenses (OPEX) + Non-operating Income

Operating Income = Operating Revenue - Operating Expenses

Operating income is the difference between operating revenues and operating expenses, but it is also sometimes used as a synonym for EBIT and operating profit. This is true if the firm has no non-operating income.

a. AAB
b. Earnings before interest and taxes
c. ABN Amro
d. A Random Walk Down Wall Street

53. _____ are the earnings returned on the initial investment amount.

In the US, the Financial Accounting Standards Board (FASB) requires companies' income statements to report _____ for each of the major categories of the income statement: continuing operations, discontinued operations, extraordinary items, and net income.

The _____ formula does not include preferred dividends for categories outside of continued operations and net income.

a. Assets turnover
b. Average accounting return
c. Inventory turnover
d. Earnings per share

54. In finance, a _____ is a security that entitles the holder to buy stock of the company that issued it at a specified price, which is usually higher than the stock price at time of issue.

_____s are frequently attached to bonds or preferred stock as a sweetener, allowing the issuer to pay lower interest rates or dividends. They can be used to enhance the yield of the bond, and make them more attractive to potential buyers.

a. Credit
b. Clearing house
c. Clearing
d. Warrant

55. In finance, _____ refers to the way a corporation finances its assets through some combination of equity, debt, or hybrid securities. A firm's _____ is then the composition or 'structure' of its liabilities. For example, a firm that sells $20 billion in equity and $80 billion in debt is said to be 20% equity-financed and 80% debt-financed.

a. Market for corporate control
b. Capital structure
c. Rights issue
d. Book building

56. In business and finance, a _____ (also referred to as equity _____) of stock means a _____ of ownership in a corporation (company.) In the plural, stocks is often used as a synonym for _____s especially in the United States, but it is less commonly used that way outside of North America.

In the United Kingdom, South Africa, and Australia, stock can also refer to completely different financial instruments such as government bonds or, less commonly, to all kinds of marketable securities.

a. Procter ' Gamble
b. Share
c. Margin
d. Bucket shop

Chapter 3. Income Statement and Statement of Stockholders Equity

57. A _____ is a financial contract whose value is derived from the value of something else (known as the underlying.) The underlying on which a _____ is based can be an asset, weather conditions bonds or other forms of credit.
   a. 4-4-5 Calendar
   b. Derivative
   c. 7-Eleven
   d. 529 plan

58. _____ is the monetary unit of account of the principal economic environment in which an economic entity operates.

Statement of Financial Standards No. 52 (SFAS 52) is the primary source of GAAP for translation of foreign currency financial statements.

   a. Currency board
   b. Devaluation
   c. Functional currency
   d. Reserve currency

59. _____ means regulating, adapting or settling in a variety of contexts:

In commercial law, _____ means the settlement of a loss incurred on insured goods. The calculation of the amounts of compensation to be paid by or to the several interests is a complicated matter. It involves much detail and arithmetic, and requires a full and accurate knowledge of the principles of the subject.

   a. Intelligent investor
   b. Equity method
   c. Asset recovery
   d. Adjustment

60. In accounting, _____ refers to the portion of net income which is retained by the corporation rather than distributed to its owners as dividends. Similarly, if the corporation makes a loss, then that loss is retained and called variously retained losses, accumulated losses or accumulated deficit. _____ and losses are cumulative from year to year with losses offsetting earnings.
   a. Matching principle
   b. Historical cost
   c. Generally Accepted Accounting Principles
   d. Retained earnings

Chapter 3. Income Statement and Statement of Stockholders Equity

61. In business, _____ is income that a company receives from its normal business activities, usually from the sale of goods and services to customers. Some companies also receive _____ from interest, dividends or royalties paid to them by other companies. _____ may refer to business income in general, or it may refer to the amount, in a monetary unit, received during a period of time, as in 'Last year, Company X had _____ of $32 million.'

In many countries, including the UK, _____ is referred to as turnover.

   a. Matching principle
   b. Revenue
   c. Bottom line
   d. Furniture, Fixtures and Equipment

62. _____ are those dividends paid out in form of additional stock shares of the issuing corporation or other corporation They are usually issued in proportion to shares owned (for example for every 100 shares of stock owned, 5% stock dividend will yield 5 extra shares). If this payment involves the issue of new shares, this is very similar to a stock split in that it increases the total number of shares while lowering the price of each share and does not change the market capitalization or the total value of the shares held
   a. The Hong Kong Securities Institute
   b. Time-based currency
   c. Database auditing
   d. Stock or scrip dividends

63. A _____ or stock divide increases or decreases the number of shares in a public company. The price is adjusted such that the before and after market capitalization of the company remains the same and dilution does not occur. Options and warrants are included.
   a. Contract for difference
   b. Stop order
   c. Stop price
   d. Stock split

64. An _____ is a contract written by a seller that conveys to the buyer the right -- but not the obligation -- to buy (in the case of a call _____) or to sell (in the case of a put _____) a particular asset, such as a piece of property such as, among others, a futures contract. In return for granting the _____, the seller collects a payment (the premium) from the buyer.

For example, buying a call _____ provides the right to buy a specified quantity of a security at a set strike price at some time on or before expiration, while buying a put _____ provides the right to sell.

a. Annuity
b. AT'T Mobility LLC
c. Amortization
d. Option

65. Earnings before interest, taxes, depreciation and amortization (_____) is a non-GAAP metric that can be used to evaluate a company's profitability.

_____ = Operating Revenue - Operating Expenses + Other Revenue

Its name comes from the fact that Operating Expenses do not include interest, taxes, or amortization. _____ is not a defined measure according to Generally Accepted Accounting Principles (GAAP), and thus can be calculated however a company wishes.

a. Accounts payable
b. EBITDA
c. Invoice processing
d. Accrual

Chapter 4. Statement of Cash Flows

1. The role of the _____ is to issue accounting standards in the United Kingdom. It is recognised for that purpose under the Companies Act 1985. It took over the task of setting accounting standards from the Accounting Standards Committee (ASC) in 1990.
   a. ABN Amro
   b. AAB
   c. A Random Walk Down Wall Street
   d. Accounting Standards Board

2. Cash and _____ are the most liquid assets found within the asset portion of a company's balance sheet. _____ are assets that are readily convertible into cash, such as money market holdings, short-term government bonds or Treasury bills, marketable securities and commercial paper. _____ are distinguished from other investments through their short-term existence; they mature within 3 months whereas short-term investments are 12 months or less, and long-term investments are any investments that mature in excess of 12 months.
   a. Par value
   b. Secured debt
   c. Tick size
   d. Cash equivalents

3. _____ is the balance of the amounts of cash being received and paid by a business during a defined period of time, sometimes tied to a specific project. Measurement of _____ can be used

   - to evaluate the state or performance of a business or project.
   - to determine problems with liquidity. Being profitable does not necessarily mean being liquid. A company can fail because of a shortage of cash, even while profitable.
   - to generate project rate of returns. The time of _____s into and out of projects are used as inputs to financial models such as internal rate of return, and net present value.
   - to examine income or growth of a business when it is believed that accrual accounting concepts do not represent economic realities. Alternately, _____ can be used to 'validate' the net income generated by accrual accounting.

   _____ as a generic term may be used differently depending on context, and certain _____ definitions may be adapted by analysts and users for their own uses. Common terms include operating _____ and free _____.

   _____s can be classified into:

   1. Operational _____s: Cash received or expended as a result of the company's core business activities.
   2. Investment _____s: Cash received or expended through capital expenditure, investments or acquisitions.
   3. Financing _____s: Cash received or expended as a result of financial activities, such as interests and dividends.

All three together - the net _____ - are necessary to reconcile the beginning cash balance to the ending cash balance. Loan draw downs or equity injections, that is just shifting of capital but no expenditure as such, are not considered in the net _____.

   a. Real option
   b. Cash flow
   c. Shareholder value
   d. Corporate finance

4. _____ or First In, First Out, is an abstraction in ways of organizing and manipulation of data relative to time and prioritization. This expression describes the principle of a queue processing technique or servicing conflicting demands by ordering process by first-come, first-served (FCFS) behaviour: what comes in first is handled first, what comes in next waits until the first is finished, etc.

Thus it is analogous to the behaviour of persons queueing (or 'standing in line', in common American parlance), where the persons leave the queue in the order they arrive, or waiting one's turn at a traffic control signal.

   a. Risk management
   b. Penny stock
   c. 4-4-5 Calendar
   d. FIFO

5. _____ is the field of accountancy concerned with the preparation of financial statements for decision makers, such as stockholders, suppliers, banks, employees, government agencies, owners, and other stakeholders. The fundamental need for _____ is to reduce principal-agent problem by measuring and monitoring agents' performance and reporting the results to interested users.

_____ is used to prepare accounting information for people outside the organization or not involved in the day to day running of the company.

   a. Financial Accounting
   b. 4-4-5 Calendar
   c. 7-Eleven
   d. 529 plan

Chapter 4. Statement of Cash Flows

6. The _____ is a private, not-for-profit organization whose primary purpose is to develop generally accepted accounting principles (GAAP) within the United States in the public's interest. The Securities and Exchange Commission (SEC) designated the _____ as the organization responsible for setting accounting standards for public companies in the U.S. It was created in 1973, replacing the Accounting Principles Board and the Committee on Accounting Procedure of the American Institute of Certified Public Accountants. The _____'s mission is 'to establish and improve standards of financial accounting and reporting for the guidance and education of the public, including issuers, auditors, and users of financial information.'

The _____ is not a governmental body.

a. KPMG
b. Financial Accounting Standards Board
c. Federal Deposit Insurance Corporation
d. World Congress of Accountants

7. _____ are formal records of a business' financial activities.

_____ provide an overview of a business' financial condition in both short and long term. There are four basic _____:

1. **Balance sheet**: also referred to as statement of financial position or condition, reports on a company's assets, liabilities, and net equity as of a given point in time.
2. **Income statement**: also referred to as Profit and Loss statement (or a 'P'L'), reports on a company's income, expenses, and profits over a period of time.
3. **Statement of retained earnings**: explains the changes in a company's retained earnings over the reporting period.
4. **Statement of cash flows**: reports on a company's cash flow activities, particularly its operating, investing and financing activities.

a. Statement on Auditing Standards No. 70: Service Organizations
b. Notes to the Financial Statements
c. Financial statements
d. Statement of retained earnings

8. _____ is a list for goods and materials held available in stock by a business. It is also used for a list of the contents of a household and for a list for testamentary purposes of the possessions of someone who has died. In accounting _____ is considered an asset.

a. ABN Amro
b. Inventory
c. A Random Walk Down Wall Street
d. AAB

9. _____ or financing is to provide capital (funds), which means money for a project, a person, a business or any other private or public institutions.

Those funds can be allocated for either short term or long term purposes. The health fund is a new way of _____ private healthcare centers.

a. Synthetic CDO
b. Proxy fight
c. Product life cycle
d. Funding

10. In financial accounting, a _____ or statement of cash flows is a financial statement that shows a company's flow of cash. The money coming into the business is called cash inflow, and money going out from the business is called cash outflow. The statement shows how changes in balance sheet and income accounts affect cash and cash equivalents, and breaks the analysis down to operating, investing, and financing activities.
a. Cash flow statement
b. 4-4-5 Calendar
c. 529 plan
d. 7-Eleven

11. _____ is an investment paradigm that derives from the ideas on investment and speculation that Ben Graham ' David Dodd began teaching at Columbia Business School in 1928 and subsequently developed in their 1934 text Security Analysis. Although _____ has taken many forms since its inception, it generally involves buying securities whose shares appear underpriced by some form(s) of fundamental analysis. As examples, such securities may be stock in public companies that trade at discounts to book value or tangible book value, have high dividend yields, have low price-to-earning multiples or have low price-to-book ratios.
a. 529 plan
b. 4-4-5 Calendar
c. Quality investing
d. Value investing

Chapter 4. Statement of Cash Flows

12. In business and accounting, _____s are everything of value that is owned by a person or company. The balance sheet of a firm records the monetary value of the _____s owned by the firm. The two major _____ classes are tangible _____s and intangible _____s.
   a. Asset
   b. Income
   c. Accounts payable
   d. EBITDA

13. A _____ is a payment made by a corporation to its shareholder members. When a corporation earns a profit or surplus, that money can be put to two uses: it can either be re-invested in the business (called retained earnings), or it can be paid to the shareholders as a _____. Many corporations retain a portion of their earnings and pay the remainder as a _____.
   a. Dividend puzzle
   b. Dividend yield
   c. Special dividend
   d. Dividend

14. _____, refers to consumption opportunity gained by an entity within a specified time frame, which is generally expressed in monetary terms. However, for households and individuals, '_____ is the sum of all the wages, salaries, profits, interests payments, rents and other forms of earnings received... in a given period of time.' For firms, _____ generally refers to net-profit: what remains of revenue after expenses have been subtracted.
   a. OIBDA
   b. Accrual
   c. Annual report
   d. Income

15. An _____ is a tax levied on the financial income of people, corporations, or other legal entities. Various _____ systems exist, with varying degrees of tax incidence. Income taxation can be progressive, proportional, or regressive.
   a. Income tax
   b. ABN Amro
   c. A Random Walk Down Wall Street
   d. AAB

16. _____ plant, and equipment, is a term used in accountancy for assets and property which cannot easily be converted into cash. This can be compared with current assets such as cash or bank accounts, which are described as liquid assets. In most cases, only tangible assets are referred to as fixed.

a. Petty cash
b. Percentage of Completion
c. Remittance advice
d. Fixed Asset

17. In the global money market, _____ is an unsecured promissory note with a fixed maturity of one to 270 days. _____ is a money-market security issued (sold) by large banks and corporations to get money to meet short term debt obligations (for example, payroll), and is only backed by an issuing bank or corporation's promise to pay the face amount on the maturity date specified on the note. Since it is not backed by collateral, only firms with excellent credit ratings from a recognized rating agency will be able to sell their _____ at a reasonable price.
   a. Financial distress
   b. Book building
   c. Trade-off theory
   d. Commercial paper

18. _____ are securities that can be easily converted into cash. Such securities will generally have highly liquid markets allowing the security to be sold at a reasonable price very quickly. This is a usual feature in real estate.
   a. Marketable
   b. Securities lending
   c. Tracking stock
   d. Book entry

19. A _____ is a fungible, negotiable instrument representing financial value. They are broadly categorized into debt securities (such as banknotes, bonds and debentures), and equity securities; e.g., common stocks. The company or other entity issuing the _____ is called the issuer.
   a. Securities lending
   b. Book entry
   c. Security
   d. Tracking stock

20. _____, in bookkeeping, refers to assets, liabilities, income, and expenses recorded on individual pages of the so called book of final entry or ledger. Changes in _____ value are made by chronologically posting debit (DR) and credit (CR) entries to its page. Examples of _____s are cash, _____s receivable, mortgages, loans, land and buildings, common stock, sales, services provided, wages, and payroll overhead.

a. Alpha
b. Option
c. Account
d. Accretion

21. _____ is a file or account that contains money that a person or company owes to suppliers, but hasn't paid yet (a form of debt.) When you receive an invoice you add it to the file, and then you remove it when you pay. Thus, the A/P is a form of credit that suppliers offer to their purchasers by allowing them to pay for a product or service after it has already been received.
   a. Accounts payable
   b. Accrual
   c. Earnings before interest, taxes, depreciation and amortization
   d. Outstanding balance

22. _____ is one of a series of accounting transactions dealing with the billing of customers who owe money to a person, company or organization for goods and services that have been provided to the customer. In most business entities this is typically done by generating an invoice and mailing or electronically delivering it to the customer, who in turn must pay it within an established timeframe called credit or payment terms.

An example of a common payment term is Net 30, meaning payment is due in the amount of the invoice 30 days from the date of invoice.

   a. Accounting methods
   b. Accounts receivable
   c. Income
   d. Impaired asset

23. _____ are liabilities which have occurred, but have not been paid or logged under accounts payable during an accounting period; in other words, obligations for goods and services provided to a company for which invoices have not yet been received. Examples would include accrued wages payable, accrued sales tax payable, and accrued rent payable.

There are two general types of _____:

- Routine and recurring
- Infrequent or non-routine

Chapter 4. Statement of Cash Flows

a. Accounting methods
b. Accrued liabilities
c. Adjusting entries
d. Outstanding balance

24. _____ is the process of decreasing an amount over a period of time. The word comes from Middle English amortisen to kill, alienate in mortmain, from Anglo-French amorteser, alteration of amortir, from Vulgar Latin admortire to kill, from Latin ad- + mort-, mors death. Particular instances of the term include:

- _____ (business), the allocation of a lump sum amount to different time periods, particularly for loans and other forms of finance, including related interest or other finance charges.
    - _____ schedule, a table detailing each periodic payment on a loan (typically a mortgage), as generated by an _____ calculator.
    - Negative _____, an _____ schedule where the loan amount actually increases through not paying the full interest
- Amortized analysis, analyzing the execution cost of algorithms over a sequence of operations.
- _____ of capital expenditures of certain assets under accounting rules, particularly intangible assets, in a manner analogous to depreciation.
- _____ (tax law)

_____ is also used in the context of zoning regulations and describes the time in which a property owner has to relocate when the property's use constitutes a preexisting nonconforming use under zoning regulations.

- Depreciation

a. Intrinsic value
b. Amortization
c. AT'T Inc.
d. Option

25. _____ is a form of corporation equity ownership represented in the securities. It is dangerous in comparison to preferred shares and some other investment options, in that in the event of bankruptcy, _____ investors receive their funds after preferred stockholders, bondholders, creditors, etc. On the other hand, common shares on average perform better than preferred shares or bonds over time.

a. Stop-limit order
b. Stock split
c. Stock market bubble
d. Common stock

26. _____, in accrual accounting, is any account where the asset or liability is not realized until a future date, e.g. annuities, charges, taxes, income, etc. The _____ item may be carried, dependent on type of deferral, as either an asset or liability. See also: accrual

_____ is also used in the university admissions process. It is the action by which a school rejects a student for early admission but still opts to review that student in the general admissions pool.

a. Revenue
b. Net profit
c. Current asset
d. Deferred

27. _____ is a term used in accounting, economics and finance to spread the cost of an asset over the span of several years.

In simple words we can say that _____ is the reduction in the value of an asset due to usage, passage of time, wear and tear, technological outdating or obsolescence, depletion or other such factors.

In accounting, _____ is a term used to describe any method of attributing the historical or purchase cost of an asset across its useful life, roughly corresponding to normal wear and tear.

a. Bottom line
b. Matching principle
c. Deferred financing costs
d. Depreciation

28. _____ is a measure of the ability of a debtor to pay their debts as and when they fall due. It is usually expressed as a ratio or a percentage of current liabilities.

For a corporation with a published balance sheet there are various ratios used to calculate a measure of liquidity.

a. Operating leverage
b. Operating profit margin
c. Accounting liquidity
d. Invested capital

29. In accounting, _____ refers to the portion of net income which is retained by the corporation rather than distributed to its owners as dividends. Similarly, if the corporation makes a loss, then that loss is retained and called variously retained losses, accumulated losses or accumulated deficit. _____ and losses are cumulative from year to year with losses offsetting earnings.

Chapter 4. Statement of Cash Flows

a. Historical cost
b. Matching principle
c. Generally Accepted Accounting Principles
d. Retained earnings

30. _____ is that which is owed; usually referencing assets owed, but the term can cover other obligations. In the case of assets, _____ is a means of using future purchasing power in the present before a summation has been earned. Some companies and corporations use _____ as a part of their overall corporate finance strategy.

a. Debt
b. Cross-collateralization
c. Partial Payment
d. Credit cycle

31. In economic models, the _____ time frame assumes no fixed factors of production. Firms can enter or leave the marketplace, and the cost (and availability) of land, labor, raw materials, and capital goods can be assumed to vary. In contrast, in the short-run time frame, certain factors are assumed to be fixed, because there is not sufficient time for them to change.

a. Short-run
b. Long-run
c. 529 plan
d. 4-4-5 Calendar

32. In finance, a _____ is a debt security, in which the authorized issuer owes the holders a debt and, depending on the terms of the _____, is obliged to pay interest (the coupon) and/or to repay the principal at a later date, termed maturity.

Thus a _____ is a loan: the issuer is the borrower, the _____ holder is the lender, and the coupon is the interest. _____s provide the borrower with external funds to finance long-term investments, or, in the case of government _____s, to finance current expenditure.

a. Puttable bond
b. Convertible bond
c. Catastrophe bonds
d. Bond

Chapter 4. Statement of Cash Flows

33. A '_____' is a 'Charge' that is paid to obtain the right to delay a payment. Essentially, the payer purchases the right to make a given payment in the future instead of in the Present. The '_____', or 'Charge' that must be paid to delay the payment, is simply the difference between what the payment amount would be if it were paid in the present and what the payment amount would be paid if it were paid in the future.
   a. Risk modeling
   b. Risk aversion
   c. Value at risk
   d. Discount

34. An _____ is a contract written by a seller that conveys to the buyer the right -- but not the obligation -- to buy (in the case of a call _____) or to sell (in the case of a put _____) a particular asset, such as a piece of property such as, among others, a futures contract. In return for granting the _____, the seller collects a payment (the premium) from the buyer.

For example, buying a call _____ provides the right to buy a specified quantity of a security at a set strike price at some time on or before expiration, while buying a put _____ provides the right to sell.

   a. Amortization
   b. AT'T Mobility LLC
   c. Option
   d. Annuity

35. _____ is a legally declared inability or impairment of ability of an individual or organization to pay their creditors. Creditors may file a _____ petition against a debtor ('involuntary _____') in an effort to recoup a portion of what they are owed or initiate a restructuring. In the majority of cases, however, _____ is initiated by the debtor (a 'voluntary _____' that is filed by the bankrupt individual or organization.)
   a. Debt settlement
   b. 529 plan
   c. Bankruptcy
   d. 4-4-5 Calendar

36. A _____, securities analyst, research analyst, equity analyst, or investment analyst is a person who performs financial analysis for external or internal clients as a core part of the job.

An analyst studies companies and other entities to arrive at the estimate of their financial value. It is normally done by analyzing financial reports, aided by follow-up interviews with company representatives and industry experts.

a. Stockbroker
b. Portfolio manager
c. Purchasing manager
d. Financial Analyst

37. The institution most often referenced by the word '_____' is a public or publicly traded _____, the shares of which are traded on a public stock exchange (e.g., the New York Stock Exchange or Nasdaq in the United States) where shares of stock of _____s are bought and sold by and to the general public. Most of the largest businesses in the world are publicly traded _____s. However, the majority of _____s are said to be closely held, privately held or close _____s, meaning that no ready market exists for the trading of shares.
a. Federal Home Loan Mortgage Corporation
b. Depository Trust Company
c. Corporation
d. Protect

Chapter 5. A Guide to Earnings and Financial Reporting Quality

1. The _____ is the current method of accelerated asset depreciation required by the United States income tax code. Under _____, all assets are divided into classes which dictate the number of years over which an asset's cost will be recovered.

Prior to the Accelerated Cost Recovery System (ACRS), most capital purchases were depreciated using a straight line technique, that allowed for the depreciation of the asset over its useful life.

 a. Modified Accelerated Cost Recovery System
 b. 7-Eleven
 c. 4-4-5 Calendar
 d. 529 plan

2. In economics, business, and accounting, a _____ is the value of money that has been used up to produce something, and hence is not available for use anymore. In business, the _____ may be one of acquisition, in which case the amount of money expended to acquire it is counted as _____. In this case, money is the input that is gone in order to acquire the thing.
 a. Marginal cost
 b. Sliding scale fees
 c. Fixed costs
 d. Cost

3. _____, in accounting, refers to the overall reasonableness of reported earnings. It is an assessment criterion for how 'repeatable, controllable and bankable' a firm's earnings are, amongst other factors. It recognizes the fact that the economic impact of a given transaction will vary across firms as a function of their fundamental business characteristics , and has variously been defined as the degree to which earnings reflect underlying economic effects, are better estimates of cash flows, are conservative, or are predictable.
 a. Unified Ledger Accounting
 b. Earnings quality
 c. Imprest system
 d. Installment Sales Method

4. The institution most often referenced by the word '_____' is a public or publicly traded _____, the shares of which are traded on a public stock exchange (e.g., the New York Stock Exchange or Nasdaq in the United States) where shares of stock of _____s are bought and sold by and to the general public. Most of the largest businesses in the world are publicly traded _____s. However, the majority of _____s are said to be closely held, privately held or close _____s, meaning that no ready market exists for the trading of shares.

Chapter 5. A Guide to Earnings and Financial Reporting Quality

   a. Protect
   b. Federal Home Loan Mortgage Corporation
   c. Depository Trust Company
   d. Corporation

5. In business, _____ is income that a company receives from its normal business activities, usually from the sale of goods and services to customers. Some companies also receive _____ from interest, dividends or royalties paid to them by other companies. _____ may refer to business income in general, or it may refer to the amount, in a monetary unit, received during a period of time, as in 'Last year, Company X had _____ of $32 million.'

In many countries, including the UK, _____ is referred to as turnover.

   a. Furniture, Fixtures and Equipment
   b. Bottom line
   c. Matching principle
   d. Revenue

6. The _____ principle is a cornerstone of accrual accounting together with matching principle. They both determine the accounting period, in which revenues and expenses are recognized. According to the principle, revenues are recognized when they are (1) realized or realizable, and are (2) earned (usually when goods are transferred or services rendered), no matter when cash is received.
   a. Tail risk
   b. Commodity Pool Operator
   c. Revenue recognition
   d. Regulation FD

7. A _____ is a fungible, negotiable instrument representing financial value. They are broadly categorized into debt securities (such as banknotes, bonds and debentures), and equity securities; e.g., common stocks. The company or other entity issuing the _____ is called the issuer.
   a. Securities lending
   b. Tracking stock
   c. Security
   d. Book entry

8. The U.S. _____ is an independent agency of the United States government which holds primary responsibility for enforcing the federal securities laws and regulating the securities industry, the nation's stock and options exchanges, and other electronic securities markets. The SEC was created by section 4 of the SEC of 1934 (now codified as 15 U.S.C. Â§ 78d and commonly referred to as the 1934 Act.)

Chapter 5. A Guide to Earnings and Financial Reporting Quality

a. 7-Eleven
b. 529 plan
c. 4-4-5 Calendar
d. Securities and Exchange Commission

9. _____ or financing is to provide capital (funds), which means money for a project, a person, a business or any other private or public institutions.

Those funds can be allocated for either short term or long term purposes. The health fund is a new way of _____ private healthcare centers.

a. Synthetic CDO
b. Product life cycle
c. Proxy fight
d. Funding

10. _____, in bookkeeping, refers to assets, liabilities, income, and expenses recorded on individual pages of the so called book of final entry or ledger. Changes in _____ value are made by chronologically posting debit (DR) and credit (CR) entries to its page. Examples of _____s are cash, _____s receivable, mortgages, loans, land and buildings, common stock, sales, services provided, wages, and payroll overhead.

a. Account
b. Accretion
c. Option
d. Alpha

11. _____ is one of a series of accounting transactions dealing with the billing of customers who owe money to a person, company or organization for goods and services that have been provided to the customer. In most business entities this is typically done by generating an invoice and mailing or electronically delivering it to the customer, who in turn must pay it within an established timeframe called credit or payment terms.

An example of a common payment term is Net 30, meaning payment is due in the amount of the invoice 30 days from the date of invoice.

a. Accounting methods
b. Income
c. Impaired asset
d. Accounts receivable

Chapter 5. A Guide to Earnings and Financial Reporting Quality

12. A _____ is a measure of the average price of consumer goods and services purchased by households. The _____ can be used to index (i.e., adjust for the effects of inflation) wages, salaries, pensions, or regulated or contracted prices. The _____ is, along with the population census and the National Income and Product Accounts, one of the most closely watched national economic statistics.
   a. Consumer Price Index
   b. Divisia index
   c. 529 plan
   d. 4-4-5 Calendar

13. _____, _____ includes the direct costs attributable to the production of the goods sold by a company. This amount includes the materials cost used in creating the goods along with the direct labor costs used to produce the good. It excludes indirect expenses such as distribution costs and sales force costs.
   a. Deferred financing costs
   b. Net profit
   c. Goodwill
   d. Cost of goods sold

14. _____ or First In, First Out, is an abstraction in ways of organizing and manipulation of data relative to time and prioritization. This expression describes the principle of a queue processing technique or servicing conflicting demands by ordering process by first-come, first-served (FCFS) behaviour: what comes in first is handled first, what comes in next waits until the first is finished, etc.

Thus it is analogous to the behaviour of persons queueing (or 'standing in line', in common American parlance), where the persons leave the queue in the order they arrive, or waiting one's turn at a traffic control signal.

   a. Risk management
   b. 4-4-5 Calendar
   c. Penny stock
   d. FIFO

15. _____ is the standard framework of guidelines for financial accounting used in the United States of America. It includes the standards, conventions, and rules accountants follow in recording and summarizing transactions, and in the preparation of financial statements. _____ are now issued by the Financial Accounting Standards Board (FASB).
   a. Generally accepted accounting principles
   b. Depreciation
   c. Revenue
   d. Net income

Chapter 5. A Guide to Earnings and Financial Reporting Quality

16. _____ is a list for goods and materials held available in stock by a business. It is also used for a list of the contents of a household and for a list for testamentary purposes of the possessions of someone who has died. In accounting _____ is considered an asset.

   a. A Random Walk Down Wall Street
   b. ABN Amro
   c. AAB
   d. Inventory

17. _____ is an acronym which stands for last in, first out. In computer science and queueing theory this refers to the way items stored in some types of data structures are processed. By definition, in a _____ structured linear list, elements can be added or taken off from only one end, called the 'top'.

   a. LIFO
   b. 4-4-5 Calendar
   c. 7-Eleven
   d. 529 plan

18. A _____ is a normalized average (typically a weighted average) of prices for a given class of goods or services in a given region, during a given interval of time. It is a statistic designed to help to compare how these prices, taken as a whole, differ between time periods or geographical locations.

   a. Price discrimination
   b. Price Index
   c. Discounts and allowances
   d. Transfer pricing

19. _____, Gross profit margin or Gross Profit Rate can be defined as the amount of contribution to the business enterprise, after paying for direct-fixed and direct-variable unit costs, required to cover overheads (fixed commitments) and provide a buffer for unknown items. It expresses the relationship between gross profit and sales revenue.

It can be expressed in absolute terms:

Gross Profit = Revenue >− Cost of Goods Sold

or as the ratio of gross profit to sales revenue, usually in the form of a percentage:

_____ Percentage = (Revenue-Cost of Goods Sold)/Revenue

Cost of goods sold includes variable costs and fixed costs directly linked to the product, such as material and labor. It does not include indirect fixed costs like office expenses, rent, administrative costs, etc.

a. Gross margin
b. Profit margin
c. 4-4-5 Calendar
d. Net profit margin

20. In accounting, _____ or sales profit is the difference between revenue and the cost of making a product or providing a service, before deducting overhead, payroll, taxation, and interest payments. Note that this is different than operating profit.

Net sales are calculated:

   Net sales = Sales - Sales returns and allowances

_____ is found by deducting the cost of goods sold:

   _____ = Net sales - Cost of goods sold

_____ should not be confused with net income:

   Net income = _____ - Total operating expenses

Cost of goods sold is calculated differently for merchandising business than for a manufacturer.

a. Real option
b. Cash flow
c. Gross income
d. Gross profit

21. _____ is a financial ratio used to assess the profitability of a firm's core activities, excluding fixed costs.

The general calculation is

$$\text{Gross profit margin} = \frac{\text{Revenue} - \text{Cost of Sales}}{\text{Revenue}}$$

The _____ is related to the net profit margin, which assesses the profitability of an organization after including fixed costs.

Indicates the relationship between net sales revenue and the cost of goods sold.

Chapter 5. A Guide to Earnings and Financial Reporting Quality

a. Second lien loan
b. Gross profit
c. Tender offer
d. Gross profit margin

22. An _____, operating expenditure, operational expense, operational expenditure or OPEX is an on-going cost for running a product, business, or system. Its counterpart, a capital expenditure (CAPEX), is the cost of developing or providing non-consumable parts for the product or system. For example, the purchase of a photocopier is the CAPEX, and the annual paper and toner cost is the OPEX.

a. ABN Amro
b. A Random Walk Down Wall Street
c. AAB
d. Operating expense

23. An _____ is a contract written by a seller that conveys to the buyer the right -- but not the obligation -- to buy (in the case of a call _____) or to sell (in the case of a put _____) a particular asset, such as a piece of property such as, among others, a futures contract. In return for granting the _____, the seller collects a payment (the premium) from the buyer.

For example, buying a call _____ provides the right to buy a specified quantity of a security at a set strike price at some time on or before expiration, while buying a put _____ provides the right to sell.

a. AT'T Mobility LLC
b. Amortization
c. Annuity
d. Option

24. The phrase _____ according to the Organization for Economic Co-operation and Development, refers to 'creative work undertaken on a systematic basis in order to increase the stock of knowledge, including knowledge of (hu)man, culture and society, and the use of this stock of knowledge to devise new applications'.

New product design and development is more than often a crucial factor in the survival of a company. In an industry that is fast changing, firms must continually revise their design and range of products. This is necessary due to continuous technology change and development as well as other competitors and the changing preference of customers.

a. Research and development
b. 529 plan
c. 7-Eleven
d. 4-4-5 Calendar

25. In economic models, the _____ time frame assumes no fixed factors of production. Firms can enter or leave the marketplace, and the cost (and availability) of land, labor, raw materials, and capital goods can be assumed to vary. In contrast, in the short-run time frame, certain factors are assumed to be fixed, because there is not sufficient time for them to change.
a. Long-run
b. 529 plan
c. 4-4-5 Calendar
d. Short-run

26. In finance, a _____ is collateral that the holder of a position in securities, options, or futures contracts has to deposit to cover the credit risk of his counterparty (most often his broker.) This risk can arise if the holder has done any of the following:

- borrowed cash from the counterparty to buy securities or options,
- sold securities or options short, or
- entered into a futures contract.

The collateral can be in the form of cash or securities, and it is deposited in a _____ account. On U.S. futures exchanges, '_____' was formally called performance bond.

_____ buying is buying securities with cash borrowed from a broker, using other securities as collateral.

a. Share
b. Credit
c. Procter ' Gamble
d. Margin

27. _____ is the difference between price and the costs of bringing to market whatever it is that is accounted as an enterprise (whether by harvest, extraction, manufacture, or purchase) in terms of the component costs of delivered goods and/or services and any operating or other expenses.

A key difficulty in measuring profit is in defining costs. Pure economic monetary profits can be zero or negative even in competitive equilibrium when accounted monetized costs exceed monetized price.

a. AAB
b. A Random Walk Down Wall Street
c. Accounting profit
d. Economic profit

28. _____, Net Margin, Net _____ or Net Profit Ratio all refer to a measure of profitability. It is calculated using a formula and written as a percentage or a number.

$$\text{Net profit margin} = \frac{\text{Net profit after taxes}}{\text{Net Sales}}$$

The _____ is mostly used for internal comparison.

a. 4-4-5 Calendar
b. Profit maximization
c. Net profit margin
d. Profit margin

29. In business and accounting, _____s are everything of value that is owned by a person or company. The balance sheet of a firm records the monetary value of the _____s owned by the firm. The two major _____ classes are tangible _____s and intangible _____s.

a. Accounts payable
b. Income
c. EBITDA
d. Asset

30. _____ is a term used in accounting, economics and finance to spread the cost of an asset over the span of several years.

In simple words we can say that _____ is the reduction in the value of an asset due to usage, passage of time, wear and tear, technological outdating or obsolescence, depletion or other such factors.

In accounting, _____ is a term used to describe any method of attributing the historical or purchase cost of an asset across its useful life, roughly corresponding to normal wear and tear.

Chapter 5. A Guide to Earnings and Financial Reporting Quality

   a. Deferred financing costs
   b. Matching principle
   c. Bottom line
   d. Depreciation

31. _____ plant, and equipment, is a term used in accountancy for assets and property which cannot easily be converted into cash. This can be compared with current assets such as cash or bank accounts, which are described as liquid assets. In most cases, only tangible assets are referred to as fixed.
   a. Percentage of Completion
   b. Remittance advice
   c. Petty cash
   d. Fixed asset

32. _____ refers to any one of several methods by which a company, for 'financial accounting' and/or tax purposes, depreciates a fixed asset in such a way that the amount of depreciation taken each year is higher during the earlier years of an asset's life. For financial accounting purposes, _____ is generally used when an asset is expected to be much more productive during its early years, so that depreciation expense will more accurately represent how much of an asset's usefulness is being used up each year. For tax purposes, _____ provides a way of deferring corporate income taxes by reducing taxable income in current years, in exchange for increased taxable income in future years.
   a. Accelerated Depreciation
   b. A Random Walk Down Wall Street
   c. ABN Amro
   d. AAB

33. Depreciation methods that provide for a higher depreciation charge in the first year of an asset's life and gradually decreasing charges in subsequent years are called accelerated depreciation methods. This may be a more realistic reflection of an asset's actual expected benefit from the use of the asset: many assets are most useful when they are new. One popular accelerated method is the declining-balance method. Under this method the Book Value is multiplied by a fixed rate.

The most common rate used is double the straight-line rate. For this reason, this technique is referred to as the _____. To illustrate, suppose a business has an asset with $1,000 Original Cost, $100 Salvage Value, and 5 years useful life. First, calculate straight-line depreciation rate. Since the asset has 5 years useful life, the straight-line depreciation rate equals (100% / 5) 20% per year. With _____, as the name suggests, double that rate, or 40% depreciation rate is used.

Chapter 5. A Guide to Earnings and Financial Reporting Quality 85

   a. Doctrine of the Proper Law
   b. Double-declining-balance method
   c. Database auditing
   d. The Goodyear Tire ' Rubber Company

34. The role of the _____ is to issue accounting standards in the United Kingdom. It is recognised for that purpose under the Companies Act 1985. It took over the task of setting accounting standards from the Accounting Standards Committee (ASC) in 1990.
   a. AAB
   b. ABN Amro
   c. Accounting Standards Board
   d. A Random Walk Down Wall Street

35. _____ is the field of accountancy concerned with the preparation of financial statements for decision makers, such as stockholders, suppliers, banks, employees, government agencies, owners, and other stakeholders. The fundamental need for _____ is to reduce principal-agent problem by measuring and monitoring agents' performance and reporting the results to interested users.

_____ is used to prepare accounting information for people outside the organization or not involved in the day to day running of the company.

   a. 529 plan
   b. Financial Accounting
   c. 7-Eleven
   d. 4-4-5 Calendar

36. The _____ is a private, not-for-profit organization whose primary purpose is to develop generally accepted accounting principles (GAAP) within the United States in the public's interest. The Securities and Exchange Commission (SEC) designated the _____ as the organization responsible for setting accounting standards for public companies in the U.S. It was created in 1973, replacing the Accounting Principles Board and the Committee on Accounting Procedure of the American Institute of Certified Public Accountants. The _____'s mission is 'to establish and improve standards of financial accounting and reporting for the guidance and education of the public, including issuers, auditors, and users of financial information.'

The _____ is not a governmental body.

a. KPMG
b. Financial Accounting Standards Board
c. Federal Deposit Insurance Corporation
d. World Congress of Accountants

37. In financial accounting, the term _____ is most commonly used to describe any part of shareholders' equity, except for basic share capital. Sometimes, the term is used instead of the term provision; such a use, however, is inconsistent with the terminology suggested by International Accounting Standards Board. For more information about provisions, see provision (accounting.)

a. Treasury stock
b. Closing entries
c. FIFO and LIFO accounting
d. Reserve

38. In finance, a _____ or accounting ratio is a ratio of two selected numerical values taken from an enterprise's financial statements. There are many standard ratios used to try to evaluate the overall financial condition of a corporation or other organization. They may be used by managers within a firm, by current and potential shareholders (owners) of a firm, and by a firm's creditors. Security analysts use these to compare the strengths and weaknesses in various companies.

a. Price/cash flow ratio
b. Return on capital employed
c. Sustainable growth rate
d. Financial ratio

39. A _____, securities analyst, research analyst, equity analyst, or investment analyst is a person who performs financial analysis for external or internal clients as a core part of the job.

An analyst studies companies and other entities to arrive at the estimate of their financial value. It is normally done by analyzing financial reports, aided by follow-up interviews with company representatives and industry experts.

a. Purchasing manager
b. Portfolio manager
c. Stockbroker
d. Financial Analyst

40. _____ is a fee paid on borrowed assets. It is the price paid for the use of borrowed money, or, money earned by deposited funds. Assets that are sometimes lent with _____ include money, shares, consumer goods through hire purchase, major assets such as aircraft, and even entire factories in finance lease arrangements.

a. A Random Walk Down Wall Street
b. Interest
c. AAB
d. Insolvency

41. An _____ is the price a borrower pays for the use of money they do not own, and the return a lender receives for deferring the use of funds, by lending it to the borrower. _____s are normally expressed as a percentage rate over the period of one year.

_____s targets are also a vital tool of monetary policy and are used to control variables like investment, inflation, and unemployment.

a. Interest rate
b. ABN Amro
c. A Random Walk Down Wall Street
d. AAB

42. _____ is the balance of the amounts of cash being received and paid by a business during a defined period of time, sometimes tied to a specific project. Measurement of _____ can be used

- to evaluate the state or performance of a business or project.
- to determine problems with liquidity. Being profitable does not necessarily mean being liquid. A company can fail because of a shortage of cash, even while profitable.
- to generate project rate of returns. The time of _____s into and out of projects are used as inputs to financial models such as internal rate of return, and net present value.
- to examine income or growth of a business when it is believed that accrual accounting concepts do not represent economic realities. Alternately, _____ can be used to 'validate' the net income generated by accrual accounting.

_____ as a generic term may be used differently depending on context, and certain _____ definitions may be adapted by analysts and users for their own uses. Common terms include operating _____ and free _____.

_____s can be classified into:

1. Operational _____s: Cash received or expended as a result of the company's core business activities.
2. Investment _____s: Cash received or expended through capital expenditure, investments or acquisitions.
3. Financing _____s: Cash received or expended as a result of financial activities, such as interests and dividends.

All three together - the net _____ - are necessary to reconcile the beginning cash balance to the ending cash balance. Loan draw downs or equity injections, that is just shifting of capital but no expenditure as such, are not considered in the net _____.

a. Real option
b. Corporate finance
c. Shareholder value
d. Cash flow

43. _____ in accounting is the process of treating equity investments, usually 20-50%, in associate companies. The investor keeps such equities as an asset. Proportional share of associate company's net income increases the investment, and proportional payment of dividends decreases it.

a. Ownership equity
b. Annuity
c. Earnings growth
d. Equity method

44. _____ are securities that can be easily converted into cash. Such securities will generally have highly liquid markets allowing the security to be sold at a reasonable price very quickly. This is a usual feature in real estate.

a. Tracking stock
b. Book entry
c. Securities lending
d. Marketable

45. _____, refers to consumption opportunity gained by an entity within a specified time frame, which is generally expressed in monetary terms. However, for households and individuals, '_____ is the sum of all the wages, salaries, profits, interests payments, rents and other forms of earnings received... in a given period of time.' For firms, _____ generally refers to net-profit: what remains of revenue after expenses have been subtracted.

a. OIBDA
b. Accrual
c. Annual report
d. Income

46. An _____ is a tax levied on the financial income of people, corporations, or other legal entities. Various _____ systems exist, with varying degrees of tax incidence. Income taxation can be progressive, proportional, or regressive.

a. A Random Walk Down Wall Street
b. AAB
c. ABN Amro
d. Income tax

47. _____ is an investment strategy based on identifying investment vehicles with above-average quality characteristics.

The idea for _____ originated in the bond and real estate world, where both the quality and price of potential investments are determined by ratings and expert attestations.

Where equities are concerned, fundamentals analysis and active stock picking are used to identify stocks whose quality is particularly outstanding when measured according to a variety of business variables and financial coefficients.

a. Quality Investing
b. 529 plan
c. Value investing
d. 4-4-5 Calendar

48. _____ is that which is owed; usually referencing assets owed, but the term can cover other obligations. In the case of assets, _____ is a means of using future purchasing power in the present before a summation has been earned. Some companies and corporations use _____ as a part of their overall corporate finance strategy.
a. Partial Payment
b. Debt
c. Credit cycle
d. Cross-collateralization

49. _____ is a form of corporation equity ownership represented in the securities. It is dangerous in comparison to preferred shares and some other investment options, in that in the event of bankruptcy, _____ investors receive their funds after preferred stockholders, bondholders, creditors, etc. On the other hand, common shares on average perform better than preferred shares or bonds over time.
a. Stock split
b. Common stock
c. Stop-limit order
d. Stock market bubble

Chapter 5. A Guide to Earnings and Financial Reporting Quality

50. In financial and business accounting, _____ is a measure of a firm's profitability that excludes interest and income tax expenses.

EBIT = Operating Revenue - Operating Expenses (OPEX) + Non-operating Income

Operating Income = Operating Revenue - Operating Expenses

Operating income is the difference between operating revenues and operating expenses, but it is also sometimes used as a synonym for EBIT and operating profit. This is true if the firm has no non-operating income.

a. ABN Amro
b. A Random Walk Down Wall Street
c. AAB
d. Earnings before interest and taxes

51. _____ are the earnings returned on the initial investment amount.

In the US, the Financial Accounting Standards Board (FASB) requires companies' income statements to report _____ for each of the major categories of the income statement: continuing operations, discontinued operations, extraordinary items, and net income.

The _____ formula does not include preferred dividends for categories outside of continued operations and net income.

a. Assets turnover
b. Average accounting return
c. Inventory turnover
d. Earnings per share

52. A _____ or reacquired stock is stock which is bought back by the issuing company, reducing the amount of outstanding stock on the open market ('open market' including insiders' holdings.)

Stock repurchases are often used as a tax-efficient method to put cash into shareholders' hands, rather than pay dividends. Sometimes, companies do this when they feel that their stock is undervalued on the open market.

a. Trial balance
b. Generally Accepted Accounting Principles
c. Current asset
d. Treasury stock

Chapter 5. A Guide to Earnings and Financial Reporting Quality

53. In business and finance, a _____ (also referred to as equity _____) of stock means a _____ of ownership in a corporation (company.) In the plural, stocks is often used as a synonym for _____s especially in the United States, but it is less commonly used that way outside of North America.

In the United Kingdom, South Africa, and Australia, stock can also refer to completely different financial instruments such as government bonds or, less commonly, to all kinds of marketable securities.

   a. Margin
   b. Bucket shop
   c. Procter ' Gamble
   d. Share

54. Earnings before interest, taxes, depreciation and amortization (_____) is a non-GAAP metric that can be used to evaluate a company's profitability.

　　　　_____ = Operating Revenue - Operating Expenses + Other Revenue

Its name comes from the fact that Operating Expenses do not include interest, taxes, or amortization. _____ is not a defined measure according to Generally Accepted Accounting Principles (GAAP), and thus can be calculated however a company wishes.

   a. EBITDA
   b. Accounts payable
   c. Invoice processing
   d. Accrual

55. The term _____ is a term applied to practices that are perfunctory, or seek to satisfy the minimum requirements or to conform to a convention or doctrine. It has different meanings in different fields.

In accounting, _____ earnings are those earnings of companies in addition to actual earnings calculated under the Generally Accepted Accounting Principles (GAAP) in their quarterly and yearly financial reports.

   a. Deferred income
   b. Deferred financing costs
   c. Long-term liabilities
   d. Pro forma

56. In accounting and finance, _____ is the portion of receivables that can no longer be collected, typically from accounts receivable or loans. _____ in accounting is considered an expense.

There are two methods to account for _____:

1. Direct write off method (Non - GAAP)

A receivable which is not considered collectible is charged directly to the income statement.

1. Allowance method (GAAP)

An estimate is made at the end of each fiscal year of the amount of _____. This is then accumulated in a provision which is then used to reduce specific receivable accounts as and when necessary.

a. 4-4-5 Calendar
b. Tax expense
c. 529 plan
d. Bad debt

57. In financial accounting, a _____ or statement of financial position is a summary of a person's or organization's balances. Assets, liabilities and ownership equity are listed as of a specific date, such as the end of its financial year. A _____ is often described as a snapshot of a company's financial condition.
a. Statement on Auditing Standards No. 70: Service Organizations
b. Financial statements
c. Statement of retained earnings
d. Balance sheet

Chapter 5. A Guide to Earnings and Financial Reporting Quality

58. The term _____ has three unrelated technical definitions, and is also used in a variety of non-technical ways.

   - In financial economics, it refers to any asset used to make money, as opposed to assets used for personal enjoyment or consumption. This is an important distinction because two people can disagree sharply about the value of personal assets, one person might think a sports car is more valuable than a pickup truck, another person might have the opposite taste. But if an asset is held for the purpose of making money, taste has nothing to do with it, only differences of opinion about how much money the asset will produce. With the further assumption that people agree on the probability distribution of future cash flows, it is possible to have an objective _____ pricing model. Even without the assumption of agreement, it is possible to set rational limits on _____ value.
   - In governmental accounting, it is defined as any asset used in operations with an initial useful life extending beyond one reporting period. Generally, government managers have a 'stewardship' duty to maintain _____s under their control. See International Public Sector Accounting Standards for details.
   - In US tax accounting, it is defined as any property other than a list of exceptions. The main exceptions are anything held for sale, and any real estate or depreciable property used in business. Almost everything you own and use for personal purposes, pleasure or investment is a _____. If something is a _____ for tax purposes, gains or losses on sale or disposition are capital gains or capital losses. For individuals, however, capital losses on property held for personal use are generally not deductible. See the IRS publication Tax Facts about Capital Gains and Losses for details.

A well-known financial accounting textbook advises that the term be avoided except in tax accounting because it is used in so many different senses, not all of them well-defined. For example it is often used as a synonym for fixed assets or for investments in securities.

A common non-technical usage occurs when people ask that employees or the environment or something else be treated as a _____.

   a. Settlement date
   b. Solvency
   c. Political risk
   d. Capital asset

Chapter 6. The Analysis of Financial Statements

1. In finance, _____ refers to the way a corporation finances its assets through some combination of equity, debt, or hybrid securities. A firm's _____ is then the composition or 'structure' of its liabilities. For example, a firm that sells $20 billion in equity and $80 billion in debt is said to be 20% equity-financed and 80% debt-financed.
   a. Rights issue
   b. Market for corporate control
   c. Capital structure
   d. Book building

2. _____ are formal records of a business' financial activities.

   _____ provide an overview of a business' financial condition in both short and long term. There are four basic _____:

   1. **Balance sheet**: also referred to as statement of financial position or condition, reports on a company's assets, liabilities, and net equity as of a given point in time.
   2. **Income statement**: also referred to as Profit and Loss statement (or a 'P'L'), reports on a company's income, expenses, and profits over a period of time.
   3. **Statement of retained earnings**: explains the changes in a company's retained earnings over the reporting period.
   4. **Statement of cash flows**: reports on a company's cash flow activities, particularly its operating, investing and financing activities.

   a. Statement of retained earnings
   b. Financial statements
   c. Notes to the Financial Statements
   d. Statement on Auditing Standards No. 70: Service Organizations

3. A _____ is a pool of assets forming an independent legal entity that are bought with the contributions to a pension plan for the exclusive purpose of financing pension plan benefits.

   _____s are important shareholders of listed and private companies. They are especially important to the stock market where large institutional investors like the Ontario Teachers' Pension Plan dominate.

   a. Leverage
   b. Limited liability company
   c. Leveraged buyout
   d. Pension fund

4. _____ refers to an assessment of the viability, stability and profitability of a business, sub-business or project.

Chapter 6. The Analysis of Financial Statements

It is performed by professionals who prepare reports using ratios that make use of information taken from financial statements and other reports. These reports are usually presented to top management as one of their bases in making business decisions.

a. 529 plan
b. Financial analysis
c. Value investing
d. 4-4-5 Calendar

5. _____ plant, and equipment, is a term used in accountancy for assets and property which cannot easily be converted into cash. This can be compared with current assets such as cash or bank accounts, which are described as liquid assets. In most cases, only tangible assets are referred to as fixed.
   a. Remittance advice
   b. Petty cash
   c. Percentage of Completion
   d. Fixed asset

6. In financial accounting, _____s are precautions for which the amount or probability of occurrence are not known. Typical examples are _____s for warranty costs and _____ for taxes the term reserve is used instead of term _____; such a use, however, is inconsistent with the terminology suggested by International Accounting Standards Board.
   a. Petty cash
   b. Money measurement concept
   c. Momentum Accounting and Triple-Entry Bookkeeping
   d. Provision

7. A _____ is a statement required of a United States firm when soliciting shareholder votes. The firm needs to file a _____ with the U.S. Securities and Exchange Commission. This statement is useful in assessing how management is paid and potential conflict-of-interest issues with auditors.
   a. 4-4-5 Calendar
   b. Proxy statement
   c. 7-Eleven
   d. 529 plan

8. A _____ is a fungible, negotiable instrument representing financial value. They are broadly categorized into debt securities (such as banknotes, bonds and debentures), and equity securities; e.g., common stocks. The company or other entity issuing the _____ is called the issuer.

a. Tracking stock
b. Book entry
c. Securities lending
d. Security

9. The U.S. _____ is an independent agency of the United States government which holds primary responsibility for enforcing the federal securities laws and regulating the securities industry, the nation's stock and options exchanges, and other electronic securities markets. The SEC was created by section 4 of the SEC of 1934 (now codified as 15 U.S.C. §78d and commonly referred to as the 1934 Act.)
a. 4-4-5 Calendar
b. 529 plan
c. Securities and Exchange Commission
d. 7-Eleven

10. _____, in bookkeeping, refers to assets, liabilities, income, and expenses recorded on individual pages of the so called book of final entry or ledger. Changes in _____ value are made by chronologically posting debit (DR) and credit (CR) entries to its page. Examples of _____s are cash, _____s receivable, mortgages, loans, land and buildings, common stock, sales, services provided, wages, and payroll overhead.
a. Option
b. Accretion
c. Alpha
d. Account

11. In business and accounting, _____s are everything of value that is owned by a person or company. The balance sheet of a firm records the monetary value of the _____s owned by the firm. The two major _____ classes are tangible _____s and intangible _____s.
a. EBITDA
b. Asset
c. Income
d. Accounts payable

12. _____ is a term used in accounting, economics and finance to spread the cost of an asset over the span of several years.

In simple words we can say that _____ is the reduction in the value of an asset due to usage, passage of time, wear and tear, technological outdating or obsolescence, depletion or other such factors.

Chapter 6. The Analysis of Financial Statements 97

In accounting, _____ is a term used to describe any method of attributing the historical or purchase cost of an asset across its useful life, roughly corresponding to normal wear and tear.

  a. Deferred financing costs
  b. Depreciation
  c. Matching principle
  d. Bottom line

13. The institution most often referenced by the word '_____' is a public or publicly traded _____, the shares of which are traded on a public stock exchange (e.g., the New York Stock Exchange or Nasdaq in the United States) where shares of stock of _____s are bought and sold by and to the general public. Most of the largest businesses in the world are publicly traded _____s. However, the majority of _____s are said to be closely held, privately held or close _____s, meaning that no ready market exists for the trading of shares.
  a. Federal Home Loan Mortgage Corporation
  b. Protect
  c. Depository Trust Company
  d. Corporation

14. _____ is the discipline of identifying, monitoring and limiting risks. In some cases the acceptable risk may be near zero. Risks can come from accidents, natural causes and disasters as well as deliberate attacks from an adversary.
  a. FIFO
  b. 4-4-5 Calendar
  c. Penny stock
  d. Risk Management

15. Depreciation methods that provide for a higher depreciation charge in the first year of an asset's life and gradually decreasing charges in subsequent years are called accelerated depreciation methods. This may be a more realistic reflection of an asset's actual expected benefit from the use of the asset: many assets are most useful when they are new. One popular accelerated method is the declining-balance method. Under this method the Book Value is multiplied by a fixed rate.

The most common rate used is double the straight-line rate. For this reason, this technique is referred to as the _____. To illustrate, suppose a business has an asset with $1,000 Original Cost, $100 Salvage Value, and 5 years useful life. First, calculate straight-line depreciation rate. Since the asset has 5 years useful life, the straight-line depreciation rate equals (100% / 5) 20% per year. With _____, as the name suggests, double that rate, or 40% depreciation rate is used.

a. Database auditing
b. The Goodyear Tire ' Rubber Company
c. Doctrine of the Proper Law
d. Double-declining-balance method

16. In financial accounting, a _____ or statement of financial position is a summary of a person's or organization's balances. Assets, liabilities and ownership equity are listed as of a specific date, such as the end of its financial year. A _____ is often described as a snapshot of a company's financial condition.
a. Balance sheet
b. Financial statements
c. Statement on Auditing Standards No. 70: Service Organizations
d. Statement of retained earnings

17. In finance, a _____ or accounting ratio is a ratio of two selected numerical values taken from an enterprise's financial statements. There are many standard ratios used to try to evaluate the overall financial condition of a corporation or other organization. They may be used by managers within a firm, by current and potential shareholders (owners) of a firm, and by a firm's creditors. Security analysts use these to compare the strengths and weaknesses in various companies.
a. Return on capital employed
b. Sustainable growth rate
c. Price/cash flow ratio
d. Financial ratio

18. _____ is a list for goods and materials held available in stock by a business. It is also used for a list of the contents of a household and for a list for testamentary purposes of the possessions of someone who has died. In accounting _____ is considered an asset.
a. A Random Walk Down Wall Street
b. AAB
c. Inventory
d. ABN Amro

19. In finance, _____ (or gearing) is borrowing money to supplement existing funds for investment in such a way that the potential positive or negative outcome is magnified and/or enhanced. It generally refers to using borrowed funds, or debt, so as to attempt to increase the returns to equity. Deleveraging is the action of reducing borrowings.

Chapter 6. The Analysis of Financial Statements

a. Limited partnership
b. Financial endowment
c. Pension fund
d. Leverage

20. _____ is a measure of the ability of a debtor to pay their debts as and when they fall due. It is usually expressed as a ratio or a percentage of current liabilities.

For a corporation with a published balance sheet there are various ratios used to calculate a measure of liquidity.

a. Operating leverage
b. Invested capital
c. Operating profit margin
d. Accounting liquidity

21. _____, refers to consumption opportunity gained by an entity within a specified time frame, which is generally expressed in monetary terms. However, for households and individuals, '_____ is the sum of all the wages, salaries, profits, interests payments, rents and other forms of earnings received... in a given period of time.' For firms, _____ generally refers to net-profit: what remains of revenue after expenses have been subtracted.

a. Income
b. Annual report
c. OIBDA
d. Accrual

22. An _____ is a financial statement for companies that indicates how Revenue is transformed into net income The purpose of the _____ is to show managers and investors whether the company made or lost money during the period being reported.

The important thing to remember about an _____ is that it represents a period of time.

a. A Random Walk Down Wall Street
b. Income statement
c. ABN Amro
d. AAB

23. _____ is one of a series of accounting transactions dealing with the billing of customers who owe money to a person, company or organization for goods and services that have been provided to the customer. In most business entities this is typically done by generating an invoice and mailing or electronically delivering it to the customer, who in turn must pay it within an established timeframe called credit or payment terms.

An example of a common payment term is Net 30, meaning payment is due in the amount of the invoice 30 days from the date of invoice.

a. Accounts receivable
b. Impaired asset
c. Income
d. Accounting methods

24. The _____ is a financial ratio that measures whether or not a firm has enough resources to pay its debts over the next 12 months. It compares a firm's current assets to its current liabilities. It is expressed as follows:

$$\text{Current ratio} = \frac{\text{Current Assets}}{\text{Current Liabilities}}$$

For example, if WXY Company's current assets are $50,000,000 and its current liabilities are $40,000,000, then its _____ would be $50,000,000 divided by $40,000,000, which equals 1.25.

a. Sustainable growth rate
b. Current ratio
c. PEG ratio
d. Debt service coverage ratio

25. _____ is the balance of the amounts of cash being received and paid by a business during a defined period of time, sometimes tied to a specific project. Measurement of _____ can be used

- to evaluate the state or performance of a business or project.
- to determine problems with liquidity. Being profitable does not necessarily mean being liquid. A company can fail because of a shortage of cash, even while profitable.
- to generate project rate of returns. The time of _____s into and out of projects are used as inputs to financial models such as internal rate of return, and net present value.
- to examine income or growth of a business when it is believed that accrual accounting concepts do not represent economic realities. Alternately, _____ can be used to 'validate' the net income generated by accrual accounting.

_____ as a generic term may be used differently depending on context, and certain _____ definitions may be adapted by analysts and users for their own uses. Common terms include operating _____ and free _____.

Chapter 6. The Analysis of Financial Statements

_____s can be classified into:

1. Operational _____s: Cash received or expended as a result of the company's core business activities.
2. Investment _____s: Cash received or expended through capital expenditure, investments or acquisitions.
3. Financing _____s: Cash received or expended as a result of financial activities, such as interests and dividends.

All three together - the net _____ - are necessary to reconcile the beginning cash balance to the ending cash balance. Loan draw downs or equity injections, that is just shifting of capital but no expenditure as such, are not considered in the net _____.

a. Corporate finance
b. Real option
c. Cash flow
d. Shareholder value

26. In finance, the Acid-test or _____ or liquid ratio measures the ability of a company to use its near cash or quick assets to immediately extinguish or retire its current liabilities. Quick assets include those current assets that presumably can be quickly converted to cash at close to their book values.

Generally, the acid test ratio should be 1:1 or better, however this varies widely by industry.

a. Net assets
b. Financial ratio
c. P/E ratio
d. Quick ratio

27. _____ or accounting is the system of recording, verifying, and reporting of the value of assets, liabilities, income, and expenses in the books of account (ledger) to which debit and credit entries (recognizing transactions) are chronologically posted to record changes in value Such financial information is primarily used by lenders, managers, investors, tax authorities and other decision makers to make resource allocation decisions between and within companies, organizations, and public agencies. Accounting has been defined by the AICPA as ' The art of recording, classifying, and summarizing in a significant manner and in terms of money, transactions and events which are, in part at least, of financial character, and interpreting the results thereof.'

Financial accounting is one branch of accounting and historically has involved processes by which financial information about a business is recorded, classified, summarised, interpreted, and communicated; for public companies, this information is generally publicly-accessible.

a. AAB
b. Accountancy
c. ABN Amro
d. A Random Walk Down Wall Street

28. _____ is a file or account that contains money that a person or company owes to suppliers, but hasn't paid yet (a form of debt.) When you receive an invoice you add it to the file, and then you remove it when you pay. Thus, the A/P is a form of credit that suppliers offer to their purchasers by allowing them to pay for a product or service after it has already been received.

a. Accounts payable
b. Outstanding balance
c. Earnings before interest, taxes, depreciation and amortization
d. Accrual

29. The _____ measures how long an investment with suppliers deprives a firm of cash -- it is (in the generic case of a retailer) the time between disbursement for inventory and collection on its sale. Thus, the _____ measures how risky it would be to increase this investment with suppliers in the course of expanding customer sales. However, shortening the _____ creates its own risks: while a firm could even achieve a negative _____ by collecting from customers before paying suppliers, a policy of strict collections and lax payments is not always sustainable.

a. Return on capital employed
b. Cash conversion cycle
c. Return on sales
d. Price/cash flow ratio

30. The _____ is an equation that equals the cost of goods sold divided by the average inventory. Average inventory equals beginning inventory plus ending inventory divided by 2.

The formula for _____:

$$\text{Inventory Turnover} = \frac{\text{Cost of Goods Sold}}{\text{Average Inventory}}$$

The formula for average inventory:

Chapter 6. The Analysis of Financial Statements

$$\text{Average Inventory} = \frac{\text{Beginning inventory} + \text{Ending inventory}}{2}$$

A low turnover rate may point to overstocking, obsolescence, or deficiencies in the product line or marketing effort.

a. Information ratio
b. Earnings yield
c. Operating leverage
d. Inventory turnover

31. _____ is an acronym which stands for last in, first out. In computer science and queueing theory this refers to the way items stored in some types of data structures are processed. By definition, in a _____ structured linear list, elements can be added or taken off from only one end, called the 'top'.

a. 7-Eleven
b. 4-4-5 Calendar
c. LIFO
d. 529 plan

32. _____ is one of the accounting liquidity ratios, a financial ratio. This ratio measures the number of times, on average, receivables (e.g. Accounts Receivable) are collected during the period. A popular variant of the _____ is to convert it into an Average Collection Period in terms of days.

a. Return on equity
b. Sharpe ratio
c. PEG ratio
d. Receivables turnover ratio

33. _____ is that which is owed; usually referencing assets owed, but the term can cover other obligations. In the case of assets, _____ is a means of using future purchasing power in the present before a summation has been earned. Some companies and corporations use _____ as a part of their overall corporate finance strategy.

a. Partial Payment
b. Credit cycle
c. Cross-collateralization
d. Debt

Chapter 6. The Analysis of Financial Statements

34. _____ is the ratio of sales (on the Profit and loss account) to the value of fixed assets (on the balance sheet.) It indicates how well the business is using its fixed assets to generate sales.

Generally speaking, the higher the ratio, the better, because a high ratio indicates the business has less money tied up in fixed assets for each dollar of sales revenue.

a. Market microstructure
b. Total revenue
c. Defined contribution plan
d. Fixed asset turnover

35. _____ is a financial ratio that measures the efficiency of a company's use of its assets in generating sales revenue or sales income to the company.

$$Asset\ Turnover = \frac{Sales}{Average\ Total\ Assets}$$

- 'Sales' is the value of 'Net Sales' or 'Sales' from the company's income statement
- 'Average Total Assets' is the value of 'Total assets' from the company's balance sheet in the beginning and the end of the fiscal period divided by 2.

- Assets turnover

a. Inventory turnover
b. Average accounting return
c. Earnings yield
d. Asset turnover

36. _____ or financing is to provide capital (funds), which means money for a project, a person, a business or any other private or public institutions.

Those funds can be allocated for either short term or long term purposes. The health fund is a new way of _____ private healthcare centers.

Chapter 6. The Analysis of Financial Statements

a. Synthetic CDO
b. Proxy fight
c. Funding
d. Product life cycle

37. In economic models, the _____ time frame assumes no fixed factors of production. Firms can enter or leave the marketplace, and the cost (and availability) of land, labor, raw materials, and capital goods can be assumed to vary. In contrast, in the short-run time frame, certain factors are assumed to be fixed, because there is not sufficient time for them to change.

a. Short-run
b. 4-4-5 Calendar
c. Long-run
d. 529 plan

38. _____ or interest coverage ratio is a measure of a company's ability to honor its debt payments. It may be calculated as either EBIT or EBITDA divided by the total interest payable.

$$\text{Times-Interest-Earned} = \frac{\text{EBIT or EBITDA}}{\text{Interest Charges}}$$

- Financial ratio
- Financial leverage
- EBIT
- EBITDA
- Debt service coverage ratio

Interest Charges = Traditionally 'charges' refers to interest expense found on the income statement.

_____ or Interest Coverage is a great tool when measuring a company's ability to meet its debt obligations.

a. Return of capital
b. Times interest earned
c. Cash conversion cycle
d. Net assets

39. _____ is a fee paid on borrowed assets. It is the price paid for the use of borrowed money, or, money earned by deposited funds. Assets that are sometimes lent with _____ include money, shares, consumer goods through hire purchase, major assets such as aircraft, and even entire factories in finance lease arrangements.

106   *Chapter 6. The Analysis of Financial Statements*

    a. Insolvency
    b. AAB
    c. A Random Walk Down Wall Street
    d. Interest

40. In accounting, _____ or sales profit is the difference between revenue and the cost of making a product or providing a service, before deducting overhead, payroll, taxation, and interest payments. Note that this is different than operating profit.

Net sales are calculated:

    Net sales = Sales - Sales returns and allowances

_____ is found by deducting the cost of goods sold:

    _____ = Net sales - Cost of goods sold

_____ should not be confused with net income:

    Net income = _____ - Total operating expenses

Cost of goods sold is calculated differently for merchandising business than for a manufacturer.

    a. Cash flow
    b. Real option
    c. Gross profit
    d. Gross income

41. _____ is a financial ratio used to assess the profitability of a firm's core activities, excluding fixed costs.

The general calculation is

$$\text{Gross profit margin} = \frac{\text{Revenue} - \text{Cost of Sales}}{\text{Revenue}}$$

The _____ is related to the net profit margin, which assesses the profitability of an organization after including fixed costs.

Indicates the relationship between net sales revenue and the cost of goods sold.

Chapter 6. The Analysis of Financial Statements

a. Tender offer
b. Second lien loan
c. Gross profit
d. Gross profit margin

42. _____ is equal to the income that a firm has after subtracting costs and expenses from the total revenue. _____ can be distributed among holders of common stock as a dividend or held by the firm as retained earnings. _____ is an accounting term; in some countries (such as the UK) profit is the usual term.

a. Write-off
b. Historical cost
c. Furniture, Fixtures and Equipment
d. Net income

43. _____ is a measure of a company's earning power from ongoing operations, equal to earnings before the deduction of interest payments and income taxes.

To accountants, economic profit, or EP, is a single-period metric to determine the value created by a company in one period - usually a year. It is the net profit after tax less the equity charge, a risk-weighted cost of capital.

a. Economic profit
b. AAB
c. A Random Walk Down Wall Street
d. Operating profit

44. In business, operating margin, operating income margin, _____ or return on sales (ROS) is the ratio of operating income (operating profit in the UK) divided by net sales, usually presented in percent.

(Relevant figures in italics)

It is a measurement of what proportion of a company's revenue is left over, before taxes and other indirect costs (such as rent, bonus, interest, etc.), after paying for variable costs of production as wages, raw materials, etc. A good operating margin is needed for a company to be able to pay for its fixed costs, such as interest on debt.

Chapter 6. The Analysis of Financial Statements

a. Operating leverage
b. Average rate of return
c. Operating profit margin
d. Interest coverage ratio

45. In finance, a _____ is collateral that the holder of a position in securities, options, or futures contracts has to deposit to cover the credit risk of his counterparty (most often his broker.) This risk can arise if the holder has done any of the following:

- borrowed cash from the counterparty to buy securities or options,
- sold securities or options short, or
- entered into a futures contract.

The collateral can be in the form of cash or securities, and it is deposited in a _____ account. On U.S. futures exchanges, '_____' was formally called performance bond.

_____ buying is buying securities with cash borrowed from a broker, using other securities as collateral.

a. Credit
b. Share
c. Procter ' Gamble
d. Margin

46. _____ is the difference between price and the costs of bringing to market whatever it is that is accounted as an enterprise (whether by harvest, extraction, manufacture, or purchase) in terms of the component costs of delivered goods and/or services and any operating or other expenses.

A key difficulty in measuring profit is in defining costs. Pure economic monetary profits can be zero or negative even in competitive equilibrium when accounted monetized costs exceed monetized price.

a. Economic profit
b. AAB
c. A Random Walk Down Wall Street
d. Accounting profit

47. _____, Net Margin, Net _____ or Net Profit Ratio all refer to a measure of profitability. It is calculated using a formula and written as a percentage or a number.

$$\text{Net profit margin} = \frac{\text{Net profit after taxes}}{\text{Net Sales}}$$

The _____ is mostly used for internal comparison.

a. Net profit margin
b. 4-4-5 Calendar
c. Profit margin
d. Profit maximization

48. In finance, _____, also known as return on investment is the ratio of money gained or lost on an investment relative to the amount of money invested. The amount of money gained or lost may be referred to as interest, profit/loss, gain/loss, or net income/loss. The money invested may be referred to as the asset, capital, principal, or the cost basis of the investment.

a. Composiition of Creditors
b. Doctrine of the Proper Law
c. Rate of return
d. Stock or scrip dividends

49. The _____ percentage shows how profitable a company's assets are in generating revenue.

_____ can be computed as:

$$\text{ROA} = \frac{\text{Net Income}}{\text{Total Assets}}$$

This number tells you 'what the company can do with what it's got', i.e. how many dollars of earnings they derive from each dollar of assets they control. It's a useful number for comparing competing companies in the same industry.

a. Receivables turnover ratio
b. Return on sales
c. P/E ratio
d. Return on assets

Chapter 6. The Analysis of Financial Statements

50. A _____ is a payment made by a corporation to its shareholder members. When a corporation earns a profit or surplus, that money can be put to two uses: it can either be re-invested in the business (called retained earnings), or it can be paid to the shareholders as a _____. Many corporations retain a portion of their earnings and pay the remainder as a _____.

   a. Special dividend
   b. Dividend yield
   c. Dividend puzzle
   d. Dividend

51. _____ is the fraction of net income a firm pays to its stockholders in dividends:

The part of the earnings not paid to investors is left for investment to provide for future earnings growth. Investors seeking high current income and limited capital growth prefer companies with high _____. However investors seeking capital growth may prefer lower payout ratio because capital gains are taxed at a lower rate.

   a. Dividend puzzle
   b. Dividend imputation
   c. Dividend yield
   d. Dividend payout ratio

52. The _____ on a company stock is the company's annual dividend payments divided by its market cap, or the dividend per share divided by the price per share. It is often expressed as a percentage.

Dividend payments on preferred shares are stipulated by the prospectus.

   a. Dividend reinvestment plan
   b. Dividend yield
   c. Special dividend
   d. Dividend imputation

53. In finance, the term _____ describes the amount in cash that returns to the owners of a security. Normally it does not include the price variations, at the difference of the total return. _____ applies to various stated rates of return on stocks (common and preferred, and convertible), fixed income instruments (bonds, notes, bills, strips, zero coupon), and some other investment type insurance products (e.g. annuities.)

Chapter 6. The Analysis of Financial Statements 111

a. Yield
b. Yield to maturity
c. Macaulay duration
d. 4-4-5 Calendar

54. _____ are liabilities with a future benefit over one year, such as notes payable that mature greater than one year.

In accounting, the _____ are shown on the right wing of the balance-sheet representing the sources of funds, which are generally bounded in form of capital assets.

Examples of _____ are debentures, mortgage loans and other bank loans (note: not all bank loans are long term as not all are paid over a period greater than a year, the example is bridging loan.)

a. Deferred income
b. Bottom line
c. Matching principle
d. Long-term liabilities

55. The term _____ is a term applied to practices that are perfunctory, or seek to satisfy the minimum requirements or to conform to a convention or doctrine. It has different meanings in different fields.

In accounting, _____ earnings are those earnings of companies in addition to actual earnings calculated under the Generally Accepted Accounting Principles (GAAP) in their quarterly and yearly financial reports.

a. Deferred income
b. Deferred financing costs
c. Long-term liabilities
d. Pro forma

56. In business, _____ is income that a company receives from its normal business activities, usually from the sale of goods and services to customers. Some companies also receive _____ from interest, dividends or royalties paid to them by other companies. _____ may refer to business income in general, or it may refer to the amount, in a monetary unit, received during a period of time, as in 'Last year, Company X had _____ of $32 million.'

In many countries, including the UK, _____ is referred to as turnover.

Chapter 6. The Analysis of Financial Statements

a. Furniture, Fixtures and Equipment
b. Revenue
c. Matching principle
d. Bottom line

57. The role of the _____ is to issue accounting standards in the United Kingdom. It is recognised for that purpose under the Companies Act 1985. It took over the task of setting accounting standards from the Accounting Standards Committee (ASC) in 1990.

a. AAB
b. A Random Walk Down Wall Street
c. Accounting Standards Board
d. ABN Amro

58. _____ or First In, First Out, is an abstraction in ways of organizing and manipulation of data relative to time and prioritization. This expression describes the principle of a queue processing technique or servicing conflicting demands by ordering process by first-come, first-served (FCFS) behaviour: what comes in first is handled first, what comes in next waits until the first is finished, etc.

Thus it is analogous to the behaviour of persons queueing (or 'standing in line', in common American parlance), where the persons leave the queue in the order they arrive, or waiting one's turn at a traffic control signal.

a. FIFO
b. Risk management
c. Penny stock
d. 4-4-5 Calendar

59. _____ is the field of accountancy concerned with the preparation of financial statements for decision makers, such as stockholders, suppliers, banks, employees, government agencies, owners, and other stakeholders. The fundamental need for _____ is to reduce principal-agent problem by measuring and monitoring agents' performance and reporting the results to interested users.

_____ is used to prepare accounting information for people outside the organization or not involved in the day to day running of the company.

a. 4-4-5 Calendar
b. 529 plan
c. 7-Eleven
d. Financial Accounting

Chapter 6. The Analysis of Financial Statements

60. The _____ is a private, not-for-profit organization whose primary purpose is to develop generally accepted accounting principles (GAAP) within the United States in the public's interest. The Securities and Exchange Commission (SEC) designated the _____ as the organization responsible for setting accounting standards for public companies in the U.S. It was created in 1973, replacing the Accounting Principles Board and the Committee on Accounting Procedure of the American Institute of Certified Public Accountants. The _____'s mission is 'to establish and improve standards of financial accounting and reporting for the guidance and education of the public, including issuers, auditors, and users of financial information.'

The _____ is not a governmental body.

   a. World Congress of Accountants
   b. KPMG
   c. Federal Deposit Insurance Corporation
   d. Financial Accounting Standards Board

61. A _____ is an expenditure creating future benefits. A _____ is incurred when a business spends money either to buy fixed assets or to add to the value of an existing fixed asset with a useful life that extends beyond the taxable year. Capex are used by a company to acquire or upgrade physical assets such as equipment, property, or industrial buildings.
   a. Weighted average cost of capital
   b. Capital expenditure
   c. 4-4-5 Calendar
   d. Cost of capital

62. In financial and business accounting, _____ is a measure of a firm's profitability that excludes interest and income tax expenses.

EBIT = Operating Revenue - Operating Expenses (OPEX) + Non-operating Income

Operating Income = Operating Revenue - Operating Expenses

Operating income is the difference between operating revenues and operating expenses, but it is also sometimes used as a synonym for EBIT and operating profit. This is true if the firm has no non-operating income.

   a. Earnings before interest and taxes
   b. AAB
   c. A Random Walk Down Wall Street
   d. ABN Amro

63. _____ are the earnings returned on the initial investment amount.

In the US, the Financial Accounting Standards Board (FASB) requires companies' income statements to report _____ for each of the major categories of the income statement: continuing operations, discontinued operations, extraordinary items, and net income.

The _____ formula does not include preferred dividends for categories outside of continued operations and net income.

a. Average accounting return
b. Inventory turnover
c. Earnings per share
d. Assets turnover

64. _____, in accounting, refers to the overall reasonableness of reported earnings. It is an assessment criterion for how 'repeatable, controllable and bankable' a firm's earnings are, amongst other factors. It recognizes the fact that the economic impact of a given transaction will vary across firms as a function of their fundamental business characteristics, and has variously been defined as the degree to which earnings reflect underlying economic effects, are better estimates of cash flows, are conservative, or are predictable.

a. Imprest system
b. Earnings quality
c. Installment Sales Method
d. Unified Ledger Accounting

65. In business and finance, a _____ (also referred to as equity _____) of stock means a _____ of ownership in a corporation (company.) In the plural, stocks is often used as a synonym for _____s especially in the United States, but it is less commonly used that way outside of North America.

In the United Kingdom, South Africa, and Australia, stock can also refer to completely different financial instruments such as government bonds or, less commonly, to all kinds of marketable securities.

a. Bucket shop
b. Share
c. Procter ' Gamble
d. Margin

ANSWER KEY

Chapter 1
1. a	2. d	3. a	4. d	5. a	6. b	7. d	8. d	9. d	10. d
11. c	12. d	13. a	14. a	15. d	16. c	17. d	18. d	19. b	20. d
21. d	22. d	23. a	24. a	25. d	26. d	27. d	28. d	29. b	30. d
31. d	32. a	33. b	34. a	35. d	36. a	37. b	38. d	39. a	40. a
41. d	42. b	43. c	44. b	45. b	46. c	47. c	48. a	49. d	50. a
51. a	52. c	53. d	54. b	55. b	56. d	57. b	58. d	59. d	60. d

Chapter 2
1. a	2. b	3. d	4. b	5. d	6. b	7. d	8. b	9. d	10. d
11. b	12. b	13. b	14. d	15. a	16. d	17. c	18. d	19. b	20. d
21. c	22. c	23. d	24. d	25. d	26. d	27. d	28. d	29. d	30. d
31. d	32. d	33. d	34. a	35. d	36. d	37. a	38. d	39. c	40. a
41. d	42. a	43. d	44. a	45. a	46. d	47. d	48. a	49. a	50. d
51. c	52. d	53. d	54. d	55. a	56. d	57. c	58. d	59. d	60. d
61. a	62. b	63. a	64. a	65. d	66. d	67. d			

Chapter 3
1. c	2. c	3. d	4. d	5. a	6. b	7. a	8. c	9. d	10. c
11. a	12. d	13. c	14. d	15. a	16. c	17. a	18. b	19. d	20. d
21. d	22. a	23. a	24. c	25. a	26. d	27. d	28. d	29. c	30. a
31. c	32. a	33. b	34. a	35. c	36. d	37. a	38. a	39. b	40. d
41. c	42. c	43. d	44. b	45. c	46. d	47. a	48. d	49. d	50. a
51. d	52. b	53. d	54. d	55. b	56. b	57. b	58. c	59. d	60. d
61. b	62. d	63. d	64. d	65. b					

Chapter 4
1. d	2. d	3. b	4. d	5. a	6. b	7. c	8. b	9. d	10. a
11. d	12. a	13. d	14. d	15. a	16. d	17. d	18. a	19. c	20. c
21. a	22. b	23. b	24. b	25. d	26. d	27. d	28. c	29. d	30. a
31. b	32. d	33. d	34. c	35. c	36. d	37. c			

Chapter 5
1. a	2. d	3. b	4. d	5. d	6. c	7. c	8. d	9. d	10. a
11. d	12. a	13. d	14. d	15. a	16. d	17. a	18. b	19. a	20. d
21. d	22. d	23. d	24. a	25. a	26. d	27. c	28. d	29. d	30. d
31. d	32. a	33. b	34. c	35. b	36. b	37. d	38. d	39. d	40. b
41. a	42. d	43. d	44. d	45. d	46. d	47. a	48. b	49. b	50. d
51. d	52. d	53. d	54. a	55. d	56. d	57. d	58. d		

Chapter 6

1. c	2. b	3. d	4. b	5. d	6. d	7. b	8. d	9. c	10. d
11. b	12. b	13. d	14. d	15. d	16. a	17. d	18. c	19. d	20. d
21. a	22. b	23. a	24. b	25. c	26. d	27. b	28. a	29. b	30. d
31. c	32. d	33. d	34. d	35. d	36. c	37. c	38. b	39. d	40. c
41. d	42. d	43. d	44. c	45. d	46. d	47. c	48. c	49. d	50. d
51. d	52. b	53. a	54. d	55. d	56. b	57. c	58. a	59. d	60. d
61. b	62. a	63. c	64. b	65. b					

www.ingramcontent.com/pod-product-compliance
Lightning Source LLC
Chambersburg PA
CBHW082050230426
43670CB00016B/2846